MW00627148

Death the Door, Music a Key

Death the Door, Music a Key

A Girl, a Harp at the Bedside of the Dying

Angela M. Sciberras, BA.mus.hons.

Strategic Book Publishing and Rights Co.

© 2012 by Angela M. Sciberras
All rights reserved. First edition 2012.

No part of this book may be reproduced or transmitted in any form or by any means, graphic, electronic, or mechanical, including photocopying, recording, taping, or by any information storage retrieval system, without the permission, in writing, from the publisher.

Strategic Book Publishing and Rights Co.
12620 FM 1960, Suite A4-507
Houston, TX 77065
www.sbpra.com

ISBN: 978-1-61204-877-2

Book Design by Julius Kiskis

20 19 18 17 16 15 14 13 12   1 2 3 4 5

Dedication

This book is dedicated to my beloved departed Elva Mary, Esther, and John Henry. The hardest music I have ever had to play.

To all the beautiful souls who so lovingly, and fearlessly, shared their final mile home with me. I honor them until my final breath, when I will open my eyes to see them again.

"I see your face in every flower,
your eyes in stars above,
it's the thought of you,
the very thought of you,
my love. . ."

Contents

Prelude

"It is the responsibility of the musician to create heaven on earth and to create balance, peace, and harmony in the environment."

East Indian Principle

This is an invitation to join me on a journey that is not always easy, but it might alter the way you think about how you live your life. The journey begins in the fragile moments just before life ends, as we sit beside a deathbed and seek to understand this sacred process through the eyes of the humble musician, a harpist, no less.

This is a collection of stories, a once-ambitious thought that has now become reality. It is the accounts of ordinary people in the midst of extraordinary moments. People like you and me, who experience grief, loss, and the anticipation of death. For the most part though, this is the story of a harp and a girl. A girl who followed a calling to sit for a time with the dying and find her life amidst their deaths and the music they shared with her. The stories are true, based on my life's experiences with the brave people facing mortality.

As I developed my skill and sensitivity as a therapeutic musician, so too did a wealth of stories begin to emerge. Over time, I observed that many of these stories touched those with whom I shared them and amazed the doctors and other medical staff with whom I worked. And so, I have chosen a mere few of the hundreds that could be shared. Stories told through the eyes of a harpist playing music to relax and soothe the dying and their loved ones.

The stories are true from my perspective and seek to document a sacred time in a person's life. They are not restricted to one place, time, or facility, but to many places, environments, and facilities all over Australia. I have changed all names and identifying information to ensure anonymity and protect the privacy of the people who have passed, along with that of their families. I must admit though, as I write each story, I imagine the person I write about peering over my shoulder in anticipation of the thought that even as he or she rests, his legacy, her story, lives on in me, and now in you. Their lives and subsequent deaths no doubt made a difference to others left behind. Isn't that all we truly want in life? Could it be that one of the most important acts they ever committed in this life was to die?

When it comes down to it, most people put death in the "too hard basket," but what they do not realize is that in our final moments, peace can often be found in the knowledge that we made a difference to someone, made life easier for our children, friends, loved ones, and maybe even a complete stranger by facing not only our demise but also the mortality of all in this life.

In the pages following you will peer through the looking glass of a therapeutic musician's day, as well as the routine developed through trial and error to find a ritual that worked well for most people, the staff, and myself alike. It has not been easy to walk through what sometimes felt like an emotional minefield. Taking the harp onto the wards each day was a challenge, with many patients unknowingly beckoning me to move through blocks in my own mental, spiritual, and emotional life, to be able to serve them to my best ability, facing my fears, which pale in significance as I watch them slip from one reality to another, leaving me to ponder what the journey would be like and where they have gone.

This book aims to showcase the work I do as a harpist who plays intuitive music at the bedside, the restorative qualities of the harp, and the gift it brings many. It is my hope that through telling these stories, not only will the "lives" of those I have played for be honored but also their "deaths." It is my hope that their stories will serve as shining examples to others that this experience does not have to be frightening, though it requires acceptance, and acceptance requires courage.

The full embrace and acceptance of death is rarely experienced, and when it is, I have found it to be unmistakable, for one's peace seems to permeate everything and everyone around him. In their final hours, these people seem as much alive as a newborn baby, death resembling birth more than ever before.

It is important for us all to know that amazing things happen on the journey back home and that there are beautiful lessons to learn from those who are travelling their final mile. If we can muster up the courage to "be present" with the dying, many eternal gifts lay waiting for us. The aim is that if we can positively change our perspectives on this most sacred time, we may then have positive experiences of it when our time comes to walk the final mile ourselves.

The truth is, as much as we think we are helping the dying by caring for them in their final moments, we are the ones dying along with them. We die to our fears about life and death and the pain that it can bring. Why? So that we can ultimately begin to live more fully until we leave this mortal life. Every death we experience in life reminds us to live more fully in the moment, become more grateful, more peaceful on our journeys.

As Dr. Michael Barbato expressed in his book *Caring for the Dying,* "Many of us live in fear of death, or deny its very existence. Ironically, it is this failure to integrate it into our life that can make dying a frightening and overwhelming experience. Rather than deny death, we can instead see it as a beacon that guides and helps us to become more attuned to the fullness and beauty of life. Death brings life into focus and gives it meaning. It is the fulfillment of a life, not merely a culmination. Preparing for death does not draw the curtains on life, but opens them wide, inviting us to appreciate and engage life, to live more intensely and be fully aware of all that surrounds us."

Dr. Barbato reminds me to make it clear that in no way is it my intention to glamorize death. Many of the stories within are breathtakingly beautiful, as they should be, but I do not seek to play down the deep pain and grief of separation felt by the family and loved ones of a dying person. Dr. Barbato explains it perfectly when he says that "loss of life comes at an unimaginable and immeasurable cost. Pain and grief are inescapable and the strength required in seeing the process through to its completion is as great for the family and friends as for the dying person." Grahame Jones, in his book Magnanimous Despair, says, "The strength I need to die is nothing compared to that which will be required of those who must go on living."

I write this book to honor all those people who have touched my life by sharing their deaths, for the families who have opened their hearts and welcomed me into a sacred space with their dying loved ones. It is in the sharing of the stories that I hope you will find the courage in your own life to be brave enough to consider the art of dying well, and indeed living well until you pass from this earth.

The book will conclude with a chapter called The Debrief. Some of the most important work is done in this time spent releasing the events of the day. Debriefing is a vital aspect of my work, and now my life was a whole pulling together the mystery of synchronicity, the amazing power of intention and the joy of manifestation. Certainly if you have been led to, and are now reading these words, my intentions of writing a book and having it published have manifested, and it stands as a testament that indeed anyone is capable of anything if the belief in self is strong. As my father would say, "You must back yourself." So, I did. Truly anything is possible. When the time is right, and you can bear to be patient enough, follow your dreams no matter what. Doors will open where once there were only walls.

It is my hope that this simple book will inspire you to do what brings you the most joy in life and fully experience the delight of creating it with excitement and fun. It is my hope that it might just assist in tweaking your perspective of death and dying and the powerful role that the arts and music plays within it. The power of one person to make a difference is immense when sharing with joy and courage whatever gift it is that you possess.

Someone once told me that I was not wise to write this book, nor did I possess the experience or credibility to do such. At the time, learning this crushed me, though I trusted that for some reason it was not yet the time to complete this work. As I place the final touches on this project, I realized that this person acted as a sacred mirror, merely reflecting the deep fears and insecurities I had about writing a book such as this. Much has happened since this time, and it is with great pride that I complete what has been a labor of love, every moment bringing me joy, tears, lessons, and peace within.

The truth I did not know at the time was that the story had so much more that needed to be added, and it was not yet time to reveal these precious jewels in the crown of the experiences of my life. I look back and I am thankful to this person for showing me the greatest kind of love–a love found in the lessons life presents us. Therefore, this book has been both a birthing and a dying to myself. The birth of these beloved stories and the death of all that I thought I was before it, leaving me naked, bare-boned but more alive than ever before.

Michael Stillwater shares in his groundbreaking CD "Graceful Passages" that the comfort of life transpiring according to our wishes is often shaken; the sense of order that kept chaos at bay is breached. Life continually carves into, and ultimately washes away, our carefully developed and guarded selves. Perhaps this book, my book, has been a testimony of my apprenticeship in dying. The simple act of writing it has focused my attention on my own mortality. It has helped me to accept what seemed to be the unacceptable, that life indeed ends, and that it is best lived by embracing the seemingly un-embraceable.

Elisabeth Kübler-Ross, world famous doctor specializing in death and dying, encourages us to make a start by contemplating the possibility and inevitability of our deaths. By doing so we may affect many things, most important of all the welfare of our families, friends, and finally perhaps our nation. Michael Stillwater reminds us that acknowledging the inevitable can be healing. Despite incredible advances in medicine and science, we are neither able to preserve our final transition from this life, nor in conscious control of the timing. As reluctant as we may be to approach the subject of death and dying, embracing our own mortality and the mortality of others is an integral step toward accepting life on its own terms and recognizing the moment by moment gift that life is.

If this book finds you in the midst of caring for a dying loved one, my wish is that you might find comfort in these stories. As Dr. Barbato wrote in his book *Caring for the Dying*, "Whatever your reasons for picking up this book, I hope that you find something of value from which you can draw strength and a measure of reassurance while continuing that most privileged of all tasks; journeying with a fellow human being as they die."

Help me, you countless thousands who died before me. Tell

me how you managed to accept death. Teach me. Let me lean on
you like crutches. Help me to cross the threshold you have crossed.
Come back from the other side and help me.

Help me, you who were frightened and did not want to go.
What was it like? Who held you up? Who dragged you there, who
pushed you? Were you afraid to the very end? And you who were
strong and courageous who accepted death with indifference and
serenity, teach me your indifference and serenity, teach me your
resignation.

I told myself that if one could learn to die, that one can also
help other people to die. This seems to me to be the most important
thing we can do, since we are all of us dying men who refuse to
die. Indeed an apprenticeship in dying.

Exit the King–Eugene Ionesco

Acknowledgments

I would like to acknowledge the enormous help given to me in creating this book. To all those who kept reminding me that this book needed to be felt, seen, heard, and read.

To all those seen and unseen who have played a part in my greater journey, helping to bring this book to life. I hope you know who you are, and you can feel my deep gratitude.

To my beloved husband who supported me from day one of this journey. Without you, the work would have never touched so many, neither would the words in this book exist. Thank you to everyone in my life who believed in me more than I did myself and to Stella Benson, my trainer and inspiration. Thanks to everyone at Stoney End Harps for the gift of my little prototype therapeutic harp; you sent it from your hearts to my hands and on to the ears and hearts of many. I acknowledge and deeply thank the health care facilities that lovingly opened their doors and hearts to this wonderful work, as well as the staff who guided and supported me in my journey.

And last but most certainly not least, my gratitude goes to those brave souls who were so very gracious enough to allow me into their final precious moments in this life. A beautiful privilege I will always cherish.

Thank you.

The Great Theatre of Life

"Music is a continual state of becoming."
Aaron Copland

Sometimes I feel like I have lived many lifetimes within one. A life filled with equal amounts of joy, fun, disappointment, and experience, all preparing me for this very moment with you. It is my hope that my story and those of the special people I have played for might inspire you to entertain a different perspective on death and dying and the role music can play in it. May it encourage you to embrace and fully enter into the process whether it is a loved one or yourself experiencing the transition.

I have been a musician for most of my life and do not recall ever wanting to be anything else. My passion for the arts and music developed very early and has been a constant companion. I have always felt I have had an innate knowledge of the power of music, yet I lacked the understanding of its healing properties. It never even occurred to me until about four years ago when my grandmother Elva Mary died, that there was a possibility I might walk in this direction. I grew up in a small country town and was taught flute by a violinist due to the desperate shortage of teachers in the area. She was a perfectionist, and it was this discipline that served me well in later life.

There were flute teachers from time to time, but they

would come and go like Mary Poppins, in and out of my life relatively quickly with no real time to truly develop to a high level under their tuition. Many small country towns experience this shortage in high level creative arts teachers. It can often be difficult to attract such professionals due to the lack of opportunity in these areas. My teacher was an amazing woman, and I feel great appreciation for the impact she had on my life. She was one of the most professional, well spoken, and kindhearted people I have ever met, and her gracious gift of time and energy has certainly enriched my life in many ways.

When I left home to follow my dreams of going to university to study music, my family and I gave her an antique style clock that I imagined would rest on her mantle. The inscription on the card read something like this.

"As you glance at this clock, may the hands of time remind you that no matter how much time goes by, I will always remember you, and all that you have done for me."

My mother was my biggest fan, never missing a performance or rehearsal. She loved to hear me play music and always encouraged me to follow my dreams, no matter how farfetched they may have seemed. I remember as a child watching her dig through her bedside drawers and the bottom of her handbag for my music tuition bills. A sacrifice I found difficult to comprehend until recently. I am so grateful to both my mother and stepfather for their assistance in laying the foundations of my life in so many ways. Not everything was always, shall we say, rosy in the past, events and experiences that have colored my life in all sorts of ways. Let us just say that in this moment everything is perfect, and I am grateful for the lessons I have learned during my lifetime, and I am at peace with my past. My brothers and their families were also supportive, acting as a collective bridge for me to cross in the transition of living in a small country town to the big smoke, Sydney.

I remember vividly the day my sister-in-law came to collect me. The beloved family I lived with at the time was completely devastated at my leaving, as was I. Many tears were shed on that day, and the pain we all felt as I left was heart wrenching. I remain so very grateful to them, even to this day, as they provided a loving space for me to prepare for the next step in my life. I left everything I knew and loved to follow my dreams. As painful as it was, I knew deep inside that for all that they did for me I owed it to them, and my family, to do so. So, I did. As I travelled along the winding country roads towards the city, I felt a mixture of fear and excitement thinking about the unknown future in front of me and the life I was leaving behind. Little did I know then how much I would have to let go of in search of my dreams.

My brother, sister-in-law, and family supported me in so many ways when I moved to Sydney, my brother even provided a flute for me to continue in my studies when the flute I owned became impossible to use. Everyone played his or her part perfectly, supporting my journey when I needed it most.

I began a Bachelor of Arts Music in 1997, my father being a support in ways that made all the difference. Without hesitation, he helped me with the finances to purchase my first professional level flute, a crucial tool for my musical development at that time. This was the most important object in my life for many reasons. It was the key to having the opportunity to attend university, it was my way of expressing my passion and pain, and lastly, it was also significant artistically. The beautiful head joint was made by one of Australia's leading musical instrument makers, John Lehner.

I named my solid silver flute with gold lip plate Maxwell. It was my sweet little thing, my pride and joy, and I was touched and surprised to see that Lehner had engraved the lip plate with wild bush flowers to remind me of where I had come from, the bush. I promised myself after my father agreed to support me by buying this expensive tool that with every breath I breathed through this instrument I would do my very best be thankful for the opportunity I had been given. University was a wonderful experience in my life. I enjoyed making music every single day and made friends with some of the most talented and musical people I have ever met. At that time, my dream was to become a musician in the navy, and I worked incredibly hard to do all that it took to make my dream come true.

In May 1999, while completing second year of my degree, I began to feel pain in my wrists when I played the flute. I was a performance major, and at the time, I was preparing for the Australian Music Examination Board Exams, a navy musician audition, and my performance requirements for university. I found myself practicing up to six hours a day with little or no knowledge of self-care techniques to counteract the effects of stress on the body.

Eventually, I noticed that my fingers were becoming slower and that I could not play with my usual precision. Unfortunately, I had to learn the hard way to take care of my body, stretch it, love it, rest it. Just like sporting athletes, musicians use their bodies in precise and repetitive ways to achieve their goals. I have since learned to honor and respect my body, knowing that it will repay me with wellness, health, and vitality. Disrespect it, and it will speak to me every time, without exception. It will send messages through my aches and pains, anger, frustration, and ill health. I realized that I had spent countless hours practicing mistakes and wasting time in frustration. When you practice mistakes over and over, what do you think would happen when I performed? You guessed it! I would play the mistakes.

I did not know how to listen to my body, and the harder I pushed, the more the pain developed, the more frustrated I became. It never entered my mind that something might be seriously wrong until I woke in the middle of the night with sharp and agonizing pain shooting down my arms and burning at my wrists. The next day, I made an appointment to see my doctor who then referred me to a specialist. I had Repetitive Stress Injury. The immense pressure on my hands and body was beginning to take its toll, and the result was swelling that was extremely painful.

I did audition for the navy, though at the time it ended with me leaving in tears at my lost opportunity, as for more reasons than one, I had not been accepted. "Please, come back and audition next year," the head of the music division pleaded, though within moments of leaving the building I had firmly decided I would not. The path would lead me elsewhere, and as painful as it was at the time, I am so pleased it did. As they say, life happens for us, not to us.

The specialist gave me a couple of options. Either I put the instrument down for at least twelve months, or I have surgery. I certainly did not want to have surgery, so I made the difficult choice to stop playing flute and rest my body. This was devastating news and the thought of putting down my instrument was like choosing to die. Little did I know that this was the beginning of a process that needed to happen for me to truly live.

I prepared myself for a future that did not revolve around me playing flute This seeming inconceivable as for the longest time it was all I thought and dreamed about for my future. Playing flute was not only what I wanted to do, it was who I wanted to be. I felt I had nothing left to work towards, my purpose grew dim, and the path before me became a wall. "What could I do now? If I am not the flute player anymore, then who am I?" It felt as if I had become nothing, fading from existence, my dreams snatched away as if taken by a thief in the night. Without knowledge about the importance of acceptance, and moving with the flow of life, I felt as if I was cast off into a fast flowing river like a piece of driftwood. The experience of dying to this part of me had begun.

I pushed out unwillingly into the middle and let the raging waters take me. With the benefit of hindsight, this inconvenience turned out to be a divine blessing as I began to find myself doing so many things I never thought I would ... or could. My misfortune transformed into my enfoldment, and I was slowly but surely releasing my desperate need to be a musician. As this need was fading, my true nature was beginning to shine through.

I decided to start singing and play percussion, which literally opened up a completely new world of sounds, textures, and experiences. By the end of my degree, I had specialized in ethnomusicology and learned music from countries all over the world. I found a deep passion in playing this music, which then led me to performing with bands all over Australia. I learned traditional Korean percussion, Greek, Macedonian, Turkish, Eastern European, African, Japanese, Irish, and Middle Eastern music, performing with bands in folk festivals and corporate events. When I played this music, I felt as if I had come home, the rhythms and melodies like long lost memories from lives past enchanted me.

My heart opened up to behold the beauty of many cultures of the world, and it led me to a position as lecturer in ethnomusicology at a private Institute for Ministry and the Arts. There, I exposed students completing music, and music ministry degrees, to the music of our world through hands-on workshops. As time went on, the students began to understand the complexity of the music, the structures of the culture, and develop a respect-filled love for the people. Some of the students desired to work overseas as missionaries, it therefore being a part of my role to prepare them for the transition into a completely different cultural setting; to experience sounds, tastes, smells, and the arts all interconnected. It was an absolute pleasure to see students frozen with fear of the unknown, who would then open up like blossoms on a cherry tree and bloom for all to see.

It seems in West we have a tendency to separate the aspects of our lives. We go out for dinner, see a show, listen to music, and take part in the arts and spirituality. The difference is that many cultures around our world do not separate these aspects of life. Every aspect of their lives is interconnected. Music, spirituality, and dance; art, life, and breath-living and dying; it is all one.

Students would ask me in consternation why we were not focusing on the music alone. I would tell them that spirituality is music, art, and life to this cultural group. Dance is spiritual and ritual is deeply rooted in song. Without knowledge of all aspects of the culture and understanding it, one cannot discern. That was why we would learn all aspects of their lives to understand the music. I am thankful for my training in world music as it definitely helps me on the wards of hospices with a large percentage of people being non-western. There are times when my knowledge of and passion for other cultures help me understand why someone might be acting the way he is or responding to me in a certain way. It also gives me an insight into which modes or keys to focus on for each patient.

Over the next few years something different began to occur in my life, unexplainable, but perfect. I slowly began to feel the desire to become a full-time musician subside. I was not interested in music or instruments as I once was. I felt like someone had pulled the plug on my need to be involved in anything musical. I had always had the desire to play music, and I finally realized that this desire did not come from a place of joy, but rather from a place of fear. Fear of not achieving, fear of what other people thought, and deep, ingrained fear of losing my identity, and who I thought I was. Without the need for music to shape my life, I found more peace within myself than I had ever experience before. I met new people, became interested in new things, and began a journey on a new path. All things related to the healing arts began to beckon and challenge my ingrained thinking around beliefs and spirituality. It was at this time when my thoughts on spirituality changed forever.

Challenging my beliefs was an incredibly painful experience, as the core of my being was solidly set. It rippled out like a stone cast into a pond affecting every layer of my life. It felt like tearing out my insides and putting my head on back to front. Regardless, I yearned to move forward towards truth. Not the truth, but at least my truth. This truth resonated within me on every level and set me free to experience joy, abundance, and peace rather than constant drama and self-induced pain.

> *"Free choice is the act of pure creation, the signature of God, and your gift, your glory, and your power forever and ever, and no path back home is better than any other path. The destination is the same for all of us, we are all on a journey home, and we cannot fail to arrive there. God will not allow it."*
>
> **Neale Donald Walsch**

My mind was evolving and changing, and I was slowly feeling the benefits of this growth. I was choosing to live more fully, to follow the impulse within, and see the miracle that is I. The divine manifested in form, here to experience life to the full and bring about change, evolution, and joy. The day came when I finally realized that I was deeply at peace with my life, all my choices, my mistakes, and the journey I was walking. Finally, I had begun the process in forgiving myself and others for not living up to the high expectations I had set.

So, how does this connect to music? Well, without this healing, without spending a couple of years of my life focusing on other things such as life, love, healing, and surrounding myself with supportive people, I would not be where I am today. I may not have the strength to play music for those who are facing death, if it were not for my own experience of dying to fear and the ability to forgive myself. In addition, the broadening of my beliefs now serves me at the bedside playing harp, as I can fully embrace the spiritual beliefs and wishes of the patient and trust that only he knows what is true for him in a spiritual sense. This is freeing for both the patient and me, as I no longer project my own fears onto the person, directing my energy only on sending out love and acceptance.

With my newfound love of health and wellness, I stumbled across kinesiology, which studies among other things the body, bio feedback, and its energetic systems. Before I knew it, I had become a fully qualified neuro training kinesiologist, and I currently work with clients from my home clinic. In time, and with the help of my husband's beautiful daughter, I found my way back to the love of music with a newfound freshness and vitality. I spent twelve months learning and becoming accredited as a healing or therapeutic musician, and I have focused this time healing myself from the inside out, mind down, and preparing to walk the next part of my journey. I can truthfully say that I enjoy living in the now with more intensity than ever before. With the ups and downs we all encounter in life, and sometimes there are more downs than ups, I walk on.

Through my life, I have felt the energy of love flowing through others supporting me at the most crucial of times. To me, this is God, Universe, or Spirit, whatever you prefer. At the last minute, when all hope seemed lost, a way would be made and the journey would continue. I have always noticed what some like to call the little coincidences, and unusual occurrences, right at the times in my life when I felt unsure or lost. I have learned over the years that there really is no such thing as coincidences and that every person and circumstance in our lives has been placed for a divine reason. This reason holds a powerful energy, and as Cheryl Richardson explains, "When I align myself with these powerful energies the best and most adventurous path unfolds before me."

It has often been stated, and I can agree through personal experience, that standing in the spotlight can feel like you might just die. Performers have a name for the white light of the spotlight; they call it "up there." They say it is like the moment when you leave your body just before dying. In this light, everything is magnified. One's lack of confidence is not simply a shudder. The spotlight makes every hole in one's psyche look big enough to drive a Mack truck through. It does things to the performer to be "up there." Actors, singers, and performers alike experience the walk out onto the stage, alone and naked in the dark, and have a moment of anxiety. They forget their lines, stand in silence, blank and alone for what seems like an eternity, only to hear the nearby voices of the stagehands and producer whispering in panic: "She is dying out there, do something!" It is interesting the way we use language.

The intensity of the attention focused towards you can terrify the unwary and inexperienced; the fear of it can suck everything you thought you knew right out of your head. On the other hand, it can feel like standing in a circle of pure gold that gives you a rush like nothing else. Staring fair square into the darkness before you, you take a leap of faith to be rewarded by the ring of applause from the "unseen" all around you. Are we talking about performing on stage or dying here? Believe me; I have experienced performances where before completion I really wondered whether I would survive it.

Like actors in the great theatre of life, everyone along my path has played integral parts, even the villains. Remembering always that we learn just as much from that which hurts us, I recognize that even the most painful experiences in my life have been essential to my growth and development. The deeper the pain, the more significant the growth, if we choose to grow. I also believe we can learn without having to experience pain, and many people do this with ease. Likewise, I believe people can and do die without experiencing pain, whether it be physical, emotional, or spiritual. I have witnessed the difference. I like to think that at the end of my life I can look back over the years and imagine myself on a large stage looking out over the audience (spirit, God, or whatever you like to call it) who is applauding with overwhelming joy and unconditional love.

I step back and turn my face toward all the people who lovingly served me and played parts in the story of my life. I glance at each one, heroes and villains, those who played seemingly insignificant roles, and those who were invaluable within the cast as a whole. As I glance at each face, each smiles back with unconditional love. A realization burns within my soul as I see each face revealing to me the role he or she played, the significance of each interaction now made clear. I see with new eyes and feel with my true heart. At last, I turn to the villain (pause), our eyes lock, and our gazes intense. Deep gratitude fills my being as tears roll down my cheek, for my heart truly understands in this moment that without the villain, the web of life would not be complete.

After expressing thanks to all who have played their parts so perfectly, I again step forward into the bright lights of the stage. The applause rings high. I bow and I dissolve into the bright light, as the heavy red velvet curtain falls for the final time. I am home. However, more than that, I realize that I never left, and neither have you.

The Webs We Weave

*"A benevolent force of energy has been available to
guide and direct you your life all along."*
Cheryl Richardson, *The Unmistakable Touch of Grace*

The story of how I became a therapeutic musician is
just one example of the power of the life force within
us. It is what Cheryl Richardson likes to call the
unmistakable touch of grace. I believe that our innate ability
to create that which we desire is much easier than we think,
and the moment it becomes complicated, we have gone off
track. The way I see it work best for me is to write down what I
desire to have, experience, or do, then let go of my attachment
to it. Lastly, and most importantly, I need to be ready to receive
what I have asked for. The receiving part is where I often have
trouble, but I am improving as each day goes by.

As I have mentioned earlier, I had not thought too much
about using music as a therapy until my grandmother died.
After the profound experience of playing music at her bedside,
I realized that the power music held was more immense than I
had once thought. At one point I found myself at the Golden
Stave Centre for Music Therapy, which is a centre attached to
the University of Western Sydney, only to find myself feeling
that this was not exactly what I wanted to do. I watched the
therapists do their work from behind a double-sided mirror,
amazed at their patience and skill to energize, calm, and engage

children with all sorts of physical and mental disabilities. My respect for these therapists was increased, but so too was my conclusion that this was not for me.

I did not put any energy into it again until I moved back to Sydney after a time living in Kiama on the South Coast. I had just emerged from my time of distance from music and was surprised that the longing to reengage was surfacing in a different way. I began to think about music as a therapy again. Maybe it was because I had spent the last couple of years studying and reading about various types of healing modalities. I had let go of the fears surrounding music, so I concluded that my gift could be used in a powerful way to serve others. Therefore, I began to think about how I might move forward in this direction. I had just begun to learn about the power of intention, and my husband and I had already been writing lists of intentions for his work and its development with awe inspiring accuracy. We could not believe that everything we wrote on these lists came to fruition without fail, and with incredible speed. Everything from salary amounts to the type of work environment manifested to the letter.

With the knowledge that I did not want to complete a diploma in music therapy, I wondered how I might move into this field without having to do this. I sat down and wrote a list on a scrap piece of paper saying that I would like to within the next few months, meet someone who works at a hospital or get involved in learning about a different type of therapeutic music course, so I could at least get my foot in the door of the music therapy industry in general. I wrote the list, left it on my desk, not noticing it again for a few weeks.

One thing I did notice was that every night for the month after, I had an intense dream about a spider's web. Regardless of how unsettling these dreams were, deep inside I knew there must be some reason I was having them. I remember having coffee with a dear friend as we speculated about the meaning of the dream, and despite our differing ideas about it, we agreed it was significant. The best thing to do was to wait patiently for the reason to unveil in time, and boy did it reveal itself. About a day later, I remember receiving a phone call. As I answered, a woman with a warm voice stopped me in my tracks as she explained who she was and why she was ringing me.

"Hi, my name is Ms. Webb, and I am ringing about doing some flute lessons with you. I noticed your advertisement on the notice board at the shops and thought I might give you a call."

Okay, so if the fact that her name was Ms. Webb was not enough for you, get this next part of the conversation.

"Okay, thank you for your call." A cold shiver moved over my body, and I waited for her to go on.

"Just to let you know a little more about me. I work at a hospital and have just recently completed my certification to be a therapeutic musician."

At this point, I actually laughed out loud and said to myself, of course your name is Ms. Webb, you work at hospital, and you have just completed a therapeutic musician's course! I then went on to explain the whole story about my scrap piece of paper and the intentions I had written on it. She too laughed and could not believe the synchronicity of this interaction.

I could not believe the accuracy of this event. To the letter, everything I asked for was fulfilled through one person. There was no way I could miss the message through her name "Webb" and the related dreams, the fact she worked at a health care facility, and had just finished a course in the exact topic I wished to study. It was profound!

It turned out she had seen an advertisement I had placed on a wall at a local shopping center, trying to get more flute teaching work. This flyer stayed on the wall for one day before someone took it down, and despite this, she had seen it. She was also the only person who called in regard to that flyer, which in some ways was disappointing that I did not get more flute teaching work, but perfect in others. I realized that the flyer was not there to attract flute students; its purpose was to attract the right person for the manifestation of my true desire at that time, which was to become a therapeutic musician.

I should also add that this lady was the first person in Australia to complete this style of intuitive therapeutic musicianship course online, me being the second. The chances are infinitesimally small, and yet, she found me, and was an integral part in my journey towards playing harp for the dying. Oh, the webs we weave!

Over the next few months, Ms. Webb and I became good friends and supported each other on many levels, and when it came time for me to think about doing the course myself, again the synchronicity was amazing. I would have the opportunity to develop my intuitive skills, be mentored, and receive classmate accessibility and support, all without leaving my home or office. The course was perfect, and I could not wait to start. There was only one problem. The course cost over two thousand dollars; two thousand dollars I did not have to spend at that time. What could I do? Again, I had to leave it up to the universe and trust that the way would again be made clear.

Days later, I spoke with Ms. Webb about the type of work I had done in the past, much of it being in entertainment and event management. A mere chat over coffee turned out to be a perfectly timed exchange of information that would later become the catalyst for the way for me to complete the course. I had an email from my new friend to say that Stella had mentioned she was coming to Australia next year and that she was looking for someone to help her plan her trip and organize events while here.

Stella Benson is a Certified Healing Musician and Trainer who is acclaimed for her experience and harp work in the USA. Ms. Webb had mentioned that I had event management skills, and she told me Stella was eager to have me help her. I emailed

Stella immediately and before I knew it we had made a deal that would ensure I would support Stella when she arrived in Australia, in exchange for full training in the International Healing Musicians Program. I would like to clarify that I would personally consider myself an intuitive or therapeutic musician. As a therapeutic musician I am there to provide an environment conducive to benefits such as feeling calm, relaxed, and peaceful with the aim of reducing pain and/or anxiety.

This was the first time I had ever experienced a real conscious exchange of what I like to call ENERGY, rather than money. I spent the next three or so months preparing for Stella's arrival, organizing workshops and a performance in her honor. Stella spoke at various hospitals, played on the wards, and gave a workshop in healing musicianship to a group of around fifteen. It was a great success. In return, Stella gave me full access to her course and trained me in the skills needed to become a certified healing musician.

This experience made it clear to me that money was not the only way of paying for goods and/or services. I now live my life on this very principle, knowing I do not always need the money in the bank, as much as it would be nice, to achieve all that I dream. I only need the belief in the "what," knowing that the "how" will present itself in due time, and when it does, act! Never allow yourself to think you need money to move forward or create what you need. Just know it is possible for you to get it, or be it, or achieve it, and the universe will do the rest. Be the change you have been waiting for.

The Therapeutic Musician

"Intent begins and ends the circle of musical healing."
Kay Gardiner, *Sounding the Inner Landscape*

hen it comes to dying, I am an amateur. I haven't experienced it, and I think that when I do, I shall still be an amateur, possibly somewhere between frightened and terrified. After witnessing so many walk their final moments in this life, I know that everything I have not resolved in my life will come up before me to finally complete. I know I will need the help of those around me, comfort, and reassurance, and having witnessed many deathbed vigils, I know certain things such as music may help me succumb more peacefully. Through the ages, music has proven to be one of the common links that connects humanity despite language barriers or cultural influences whether it takes form as a solo chant or symphonic orchestra or choir.

The art of being a therapeutic musician is not a performance but a service. It is a service where the focus remains on the patient's needs, not the musicians and their need for approval and self actualization. This can be a difficult lesson for artists to learn, as in most cases, they, myself included, are taught from very early in their training that indeed the focus is on them, and that yes, it is all about them. Stella Benson explains the artist will gain a level of comfort in knowing that music can and does make a difference, to not only the patient, but the family members, friends, and loved ones. Similarly, staff and caregivers will be soothed and comforted, their pain and concern lifted if but for a moment of peace in a time of need.

The therapeutic musician can, and will, ultimately walk away from each bedside with the knowledge that those involved benefited in some way, somehow. Most importantly, as the ethereal connection between this world and the other, music will change us, heal us, and fulfill us, acting as a bridge of sound between life and death.

The International Healing Musician's Program, founded by Stella Benson, is an online telecommunications-training program that accepts qualified participants from all over the English-speaking world. Stella trains musicians of all levels to play live music at the bedsides of the dying and ailing, her dream being to "spread the healing" with music. The musicians receive training to provide a service to help patients relax, rest, feel comfortable, and help restore wellness.

Stella explains there is sometimes confusion over what a healing (therapeutic) musician actually does and how the work of the healing musician compares with the work of the music therapist. A healing musician is a musician who plays noninvasive live music at the bedsides of those who are faced with illness, injury, and imminent death. Their interactions generally occur in the person's home, hospice, or clinical setting. A healing or therapeutic musician uses the intrinsic healing elements of live music and sound to enhance the environment for patients in healthcare settings, making it more conductive to the human healing process.

Stella goes on to say that it is her understanding that a music therapist uses musical instruments and music making as therapeutic tools primarily to rehabilitate the normal functions of living and/or improve quality of life. A healing musician uses the artistic application of the intrinsic elements of live music and sound to provide an environment conductive to the healing process. The affective application of healing music is an art based on the science of sound. It is live acoustic music, played or sung, specifically tailored to the patient's immediate needs.

Another aspect of the training received by the therapeutic musician is intuitive listening, and it remains for me the most important part of my work at the bedside. Deep listening is the introduction for tapping into our intuitive skills, and as a healing musician, I constantly rely on these faculties. There are times when the musician cannot communicate with the patient, the patient being heavily sedated or comatose. Perfecting this intuitive listening skill can aid in better serving the patient and playing music appropriate in the moment. I cannot tell you how many times I have intuitively chosen a song to play for a comatose patient, with the result of the surrounding family ending up in tears and wondering how I could have known that this was their most favorite song. It is an interesting phenomenon, indeed.

In my experience with palliative care patients, many do not have the energy to interact with others and will send me away unless they realize that all they need do is relax and, if need be, fall asleep. Most of the people I play for have trouble keeping up their energy to stay awake while I play. Being ill and in pain seems to consume most of their vital energy, and the small amount left is reserved for loved ones. The healing musician, therefore, allows the patient to "absorb" the music and its restorative qualities as they desire or are able.

Once I started the International Healing Musicians Program with Stella Benson, it was time to begin work as a healing or therapeutic musician within a hospice or hospital. My friend had completed her internship at an aged care facility, and I thought this might be a good place to start. I wrote a letter and waited for the reply.

A couple of weeks later, I walked through the large glass doors of the aged care facility. To start with, I was given specific patients to play for, which in some ways was good. I was happy with this and looked forward to my next visit, which would be my first session with clients in a more professional sense.

The first patient I played for at this facility was someone who was unresponsive. I found my way to her room and walked in to find the woman awake and staring out the window. Even though I had been prepared and knew what to expect with this patient, I guess it was not until I was actually confronted with the reality that I found myself speechless and stumbling over my words. I would imagine this would be common amongst many.

"Good morning, my name is Angela. If it is okay with you, I would like to play some music for you." I leaned over her bed and placed my hand on hers waiting for a response. To my surprise, she turned her head and said in a breathless voice, "Yes." A little shocked she did actually respond, I stopped for a moment, collected my thoughts, and set up my music stand and flute.

At this stage, I was still playing flute to the patients. Over the next few months, I would develop lovely relationships with many of the residents at the aged care facility, and I enjoyed playing music for a large range of people from all walks of life. Most of these people were quite well and mobile, and many of them simply wanted someone with whom they could talk. One particular day, I began playing in the foyer, and before I knew it, there were over ten elderly women sitting in the room with their cups of tea, expressing how lovely it was to be together listening to the music.

This became a weekly event they all looked forward to, many being brought to tears when hearing a familiar song. They would then tell stories of their pasts and explain why that song was so precious to them. Sometimes I would hear these stories dozens of times, but I just smiled and listened knowing that for just a moment they were free to be somewhere other than this nursing home. They could visualize the past, better days, and people they loved. As one woman said, "I don't mean to cry, but I know it is good for me to do it." To be honest, I think many of these people preferred I did not play, interrupting me constantly and speaking while I played. It was quite humorous in some ways, and of course, frustrating in others.

There was even one man who followed me out into the foyer one afternoon as I was leaving. I heard a voice from behind me, not realizing he was actually speaking to me. As he had limited English speaking ability, he spoke to me in his native tongue trying to get his point across as best he could. He would speak, then sing, me concluding that he would like me to play for him.

"Would you like me to play some music for you, sir?" I said as clearly as I could. He nodded and turned around, waving his arms as if motioning me to follow him back to his room. Once I arrived, there he sat down in his chair, and I began to get my flute out of its case. As I sat down to play, I noticed he was taking off his shoe, shouting at me and pointing at his big toe. This completely confused me, and I asked him again, "Do you want me to play for you today?" He then started wailing and pointing at his toe as if in pain. At this point, I was beginning to panic, realizing that, no, he did not want music, what he wanted was someone to fix his sore toe. The lines of communication were out! In the end, I packed up my flute and told him in a loud voice that I would get a nurse. No matter how good my music was at that stage, it certainly was not going to fix this frustrated man's toe.

One dear woman continually confused me with my friend who had played harp there earlier in the year, and if she did not think that I was my friend, she thought my friend was my mother. On one hand, this was a test of one's patience, on the other, the realization that the environment I was in was not quite what I needed to complete all aspects of my training. I decided to start looking further abroad for something different. At this stage of my training, I was required to practice playing music one-to-one, using rhythm, melody, and harmony to meet the specific needs of a person. This was hard to achieve at this particular facility as most of my work was gravitating towards group sessions, so the time was right to move on.

It was not long before I was guided toward a health care facility that will remain nameless to protect the patients and their loved ones. Within a week of feeling the need to try a different facility, I had a phone call from a dear friend, Lindy, who had just met with a friend of her own. What is interesting about this is that at that time she did not know I was thinking of trying a new place. It just goes to show that when we are in the flow, the information comes to us with great ease. Lindy said her friend had mentioned a particular health care facility and thought it might be a good place to work as a therapeutic musician.

"I don't know why, but I really feel that it is important that you follow this up," said Lindy, and when Lindy says something like that, one does follow up without a second thought as she is invariably right! Without hesitation, I looked up the particular health care provider on the Internet and found a number to dial. I explained I was a training therapeutic musician, and I was interested in gaining experience playing music at the bedsides of the patients at the hospital. In this moment, I did not even know this health care provider was palliative care specialized and that this was the perfect place to complete my training. At this facility I received the support and training I longed for, and I felt strongly that I was in the right place at the right time to develop my skills.

Most of my bedside work is done as a volunteer, although there have been very generous people who have stepped forward to support me as I have pledged more time to playing for patients. These people will also remain anonymous, though I hope that if they read this they will know who they are and feel the gratitude I feel for their kindness. The requests come from patients, their families, nurses, chaplains, bereavement officers, and other health care professionals.

After a short time on the wards, I began to notice that the

flute was not quite appropriate for many of the patients I was playing for, especially those very close to death. It seemed that the dynamic range on the flute was not broad enough, being too loud in many situations. When people are ill and dying, sound can be irritating, anything, for that matter, can be irritating, so I knew it was time I learned the harp.

Again, as synchronicity would have it, my friend Ms. Webb just so happened to have two harps, and she generously offered to lend me one for a while to try it. I immediately fell in love with the harp and every aspect of playing it. I spent day and night practicing easy tunes so that I could play them to patients as soon as possible. This took me about three months, and when the time came for me to give my friend's harp back, a little therapy harp arrived from America to take its place, and so the journey continued.

I bring my beautiful little Stoney End lap harp to each location and set up as close to the patient as possible. This particular harp was sent as a gift from Stella Benson, my trainer, and Stoney End Harps, both great supporters of the development of therapeutic/healing music in Australia. Stoney End has recently perfected its therapy harp, and the harp I have is the prototype. This harp is half as heavy and comes with a strap so I can play it while standing or sitting. It was the perfect addition to my work. It is ideal for carrying around the wards, and it is just the right balance of warmth, dynamic, and size for this particular type of work in palliative care. Even though this compact prototype had a few imperfections, she was truly perfect.

The harp is easily transportable and takes up minimal space. Typically, I play from twenty to thirty minutes per room or person depending on the specific needs of the patient. I rarely work for more than four hours, and I try to spend as much time as possible recording and releasing the events of the sessions. This work is very energizing, but it is also extremely emotionally and physically exhausting. It is important for me to spend time debriefing my sessions, processing, and practicing self-care.

Before I begin playing one-on-one, I find it is beneficial for both the staff and me to play music in the halls of a facility for roughly half an hour. I have found this to be a critical time to meditate on the strings and harmonies to bring my vibration to that which matches the harp. I personally find it difficult to sit down at the bedside without first warming up. It takes twenty minutes or so for me to relax and become open to the intuitive messages I receive.

The fact is that if I do not spend this time centering myself, I find my playing difficult, mistake ridden, and disjointed. Therefore, this has become a part of the ritual I perform each time I walk on to the ward. I felt intuitively that I needed to prepare for the experiences at the bedside in some way, not unlike one does for prayer or meditation, if only to put myself in the most open and receptive state possible.

Before playing for each patient, I spend time reflecting for a few moments on the following elements. I have discovered that this ritual, similar to that used by Tami Briggs, a harp therapist in America, is essential, and I focus on these elements before and while I play to invoke a powerful energy of healing music for the patient.

Firstly, I imagine bringing a powerful force of love to whomever I play. I then focus on being open to divinely guided messages and making the instrument sing in a time and space that is not always pretty, so to speak. I use pure intention to bring about holistic healing (body, mind, emotions, and spirit) and remain open to whatever happens in each moment, being present as much as possible at all times. Lastly, I tune in and begin to listen with my whole body, connecting with the person, becoming the receiver as we develop our sensitivity and intelligent listening skills to become more aware of subtle energy and guidance.

One technique that can be used to develop this sensitivity is to begin a daily practice of humming. Simple yet very effective, humming begins our fine-tuning process, and by simply humming for ten to fifteen minutes, you can alter the experience of your entire day. This is a technique I was taught in the International Healing Musicians Program and has proved to be an invaluable tool for me in developing my intuitive listening skills. Our body benefits in many ways including bringing stillness to the mind, eliminating tension, strengthening our breathing capacity, regulating heart rates and blood pressure, and developing bone condition. The resonance from the humming vibrates our jaw and skull, stimulating the brain and body.

As many of the patients are semiconscious or comatose, this type of preparation is paramount in providing the most supportive music for their needs, needs that the dying person can no longer express through the usual means of communication. We need to go deeper and listen for the still small voice that will hopefully speak to me and guide me to play the patients' cosmic message through sound.

When these elements are present, a sacred space is created, and the environment is transformed into a holy place for the transition of body, mind, and spirit, indeed a graceful passage. There is one more thing I do just before playing, and that is saying in my mind: "I take nothing from you, and you take nothing from me." This is a type of energetic protection and sealing to ensure that neither the patient nor I will be ill affected by our interaction and that only that which is meant for the greater good will occur. I then take a deep breath, the connection between this world and the next, and place my fingers on the harp strings. For the most part, the music I play is improvised. I try to as much as possible play music that is intuitive, flowing from within. There is also music based on ancient Irish melodies and pre-Gregorian chant harmonies that are very useful at the bedside.

Creating a space is the most important role we play as healing musicians. Bruce H. Lipton, Ph.D., has now proved how important this role is and how life changing it can be for the patients we serve. In "The Biology of Belief," Dr. Lipton introduces us to the science that radically changes our understanding of life and ultimately how we live it. He has proven that genes and DNA do not control our biology; instead, DNA is controlled by signals from outside the cell, including the environment we encounter and even the energetic messages emanating from our positive or negative thoughts. This profoundly hopeful synthesis of the latest research in cell biology and quantum physics is being hailed as a major breakthrough, showing that our bodies can be changed as we retrain our thinking and environments.

For my closing ritual and when leaving the patient I reflect on our time together and then ask for the healing to be complete and sealed. I then spend time washing my hands and asking for disconnection. This is a crucial step in the physical ritual of letting go of past events that may or may not have affected us in a negative way. The washing of hands is both physical and metaphysical. On the one hand, it is good practice in a health care facility to wash your hands after being with every patient to stop the spread of infection. Additionally, it reminds me to cleanse any possible negative associations related to that experience and move on.

Debriefing is the next step within the closing ritual, and it is done at the end of the day or the end of the shift. Sometimes depending on the session, I have had to debrief immediately so as not to allow the experience to affect my practice in the immediate moments afterwards. There are times when unless I debrief I cannot move onto the next patient. It is essential.

I have been incredibly blessed to be supported by some of the most amazing professionals. In all my life, I have not met such gentle, compassionate, and dedicated people who truly influence the world on so many levels. They have been supportive of my endeavours and a vital inspiration in my writing. These people taught me that I could use words to ignite imagination, inspire, and touch people from all walks of life.

It is certainly a magical journey playing music in these types of settings. If you wonder if this journey could be a path you may like to take, be assured you do not have to be formally trained in music to receive or share its benefits. Yes, I did have formal training in music, but believe me when I say that going to the bedside with an instrument I had never played before took me to places within myself I never knew I had. The initial frustration of not having the same mastery I have on flute on the harp was a painful yet humbling experience. It forced me to step away from everything I knew about music, letting go of relying on technique and musical notation. This set me free to focus on attuning to something of a deeper nature, something that could only come in the still silence of the present moment, a communion with music, and the person for whom I played. You too, no matter if you are a beginner, professional, or have never even played an instrument can achieve this if you wish.

Over the years, I have worked with various musicians who sought to do this work, from professionals to beginners, more and more it became apparent that the music was a small part of the whole experience. The music is a key, death is the door, and you must be ready to walk through it if you want to find the power in the moments spent at the bedside.

I have met some of the most talented musicians who just could not bear sitting at the bedside with their instrument. I have also spent time with palliative care nurses with years of experience with the dying who thought they may give it a go, and after one or two bedsides decided that this indeed was not for them, feeling like it was all a strange joke—needless to say, it ended there.

I will be honest in saying that in my experience this work is not for everyone, as everyone is not for the work. That is life; we all have our unique gifts and talents, dispositions, and joys.

You may be a virtuoso musician on stage, yet when placed on the platform waving goodbye to the dying, you may falter . . . or not. You may finally find your niche. You may be a retired pensioner who loves playing music, little experience but enjoy it nonetheless. You may be the perfect fit, or you may be a square peg in a round hole. It is not to say that it is too hard to do or that one is better than another. It just is. The work is as it is, and we either love it, are drawn to it or not, that, my friend, is perfect. The point is this work is more about what energy you bring to it, no more, no less.

Whatever our experience or background, we can learn how to utilize the power of music to enhance the lives of others and ourselves. For those of you who have music experience, this information enables you to see music in a new way, to experience life through a musical world.

"True art must be heartfelt before it can be expressed through the voice, hands, and the artistic medium. No amount of technical or material knowledge can replace the wisdom of the heart."

Marja J. Schantz

Elva Mary

"My goal in life is to give to the world what I was lucky enough to receive. The ecstasy of the divine union, through music and dance."

Michael Jackson

It was a sunny afternoon last time I saw my nana, Elva Mary, lying in a cedar casket at a viewing in the local funeral parlor. Sometimes I wish I made a different decision, was happy to just "remember her as she was," so to speak, and not have the intense need to say my final goodbye, see her one last time. I didn't know it at the time, as painful as this experience was, it was my first experience of truly seeing the face of death. The face that can be frightening, upsetting, devastating, and indeed shock one to the very core.

My father came with me. We walked. He warned me that the funeral home did not expect a viewing and therefore did not prepare her in the usual way. I remember walking through the large wooden doors and being asked to wait a moment while they prepared for us to see her. Again the funeral director warned us, "Mum may not look like you remember." He felt the need to remind us yet again. Even this did not prepare me for what I was about to see.

And what did I see? I saw nothing that in any way, shape, or form resembled Nan. The shock hit my system like a freight train. Who was this person laying in the casket before me? You know Edvard Munch's painting called The Scream? Well, if you do then you can conjure up an image that may just give you an idea of what I saw. I remember sobbing uncontrollably, the devastation was immense. Where had my little Nan gone, for this was not her. This was the first time I saw the real face of death. Little did I know that this face, this look, this expression would be one I would see over and over again hundreds of times.

It is amazing how a seemingly ordinary experience can suddenly turn into a life-changing event, forever opening the door to a whole new way of seeing, hearing, and feeling. At least that is the way it happened for me the day my grandmother Elva Mary died a number of years back.

I am sure many would agree that the wonder of life and the people in it are often overlooked. The preciousness of being alive, of appreciating ourselves, each other, and our world is sometimes the last thing we remember in our rush to handle the details of daily life.

It is in the remembering of the fragility of our days, says Stillwater, that awakens us to the truth that in every moment we are dying to something, and ultimately, we and every one we know, will leave this world. With every loss, we are faced with the fragility of our situation, our mortality. We die a little each day. In countless minor and major ways we lose control over and over again. How, Stillwater says, we then respond to this continuous practice is our preparation for how we will face our own eventual death, as well as how we meet others during their times of transition.

Even though I did not feel prepared, my experience of playing music for the dying was with my grandmother Elva Mary. This experience, as if a marker drawn in the sands of time awakened within me the desire to use music in a more prescriptive way and share its power with many who experience the transition mortal death brings.

Elva, my beloved Nan, had been deteriorating rapidly over

the last year of her life, and it was no surprise to me when I received the phone call from my father to say that he felt her time to leave was near. I knew I needed to come to my grandmother immediately if I was to see her again before her passing. Recognizing the urgency in his voice and the "knowing" in my heart, I packed my bags and began the four-hour drive to Parkes NSW where Nan had lived for over thirty years. I drove to be by her side at this sacred time, not realizing the importance of this experience and its impact on my life.

I remember arriving at her home midmorning and walking up the front steps of the aging colonial style home. On looking back at this time, this action showed the unconscious awareness that there was not a moment to lose, the final moments of her life reflecting the last grains of sand falling through the hourglass of time.

I do not consciously remember making a choice, it just happened that way. For the prior twenty-four years of my life, we always used the back door, taking the long way around through the garden, into the sunroom that always held the scent of delicate sweet smelling oils and paint. Elva loved painting on china of all shapes and sizes in this room. She came to this art form relatively late in life, though brought full mastery to each and every piece she so lovingly covered in glorious flowers of every kind. So realistic did each piece become, one felt she could touch the petals and savor the scent of the flower brought to life through a sometimes labor-intensive process of up to thirty firings.

For those of you who do not know, when painting on china, one paints in layers. Starting from the pale hues of background shading to the detail contained in the tiny stamens and stems. Once a color had been applied to an area, that would be it, satisfaction of the completed product would need to wait as each firing brought the elementals she created to life. To this day when I open Nan's paint boxes, the smell of the oil brings back memories of sitting in this sunlit room, painting by her side, and watching her work magic on the delicate porcelain. Pink and yellow roses were her favourite. Oh, and forget-me-nots. It occurs to me now that life is a bit like a delicate china painting. We add experiences to our palette, colors to our journey, fired by the intense heat of challenge, given character by the shadow and shade, given depth with every layer of each day, finally revealing a beautiful flower in full bloom.

As I approached the front door, my aunt unlocked and opened the large ornate wooden door that had remained for the most part of thirty years used for the occasional visit of a stranger. I entered to find my grandmother sitting in her favourite brown leather recliner, slumped, a mere shadow of the vibrant woman she once was. The only thing that was vibrant now was the beautiful rainbow colored handmade rug that her youngest daughter Cheryl made before she died of cancer years earlier. My grandmother treasured it deeply. As I knelt at her feet, she lifted her head and gazed at me, and a tear in her fading blue eyes appeared. Recognition finally came and she embraced me. She whispered in my ear, "Angela, I didn't think I would ever see you again!" I held her for a moment and moved back to sit on the footstool before her.

She glanced up at me, this time with a bewildered look, and she seemed so confused. Her eyes had glazed over, as if a significant part of the person she was had already passed. The process had already begun and her journey was nearing an end. Or was it just beginning? Noticing her untouched meal beside her chair, and being too weak to feed herself, I picked up the plate and began to feed her. This proved to be one of the most humbling experiences of my life. She tried to eat, but it was now hard for her to swallow even a little water, her body was beginning to shut down.

Over the three days I stayed with her, I was thrust into the world of palliative care, without even knowing that this modality of care existed. I worked with home care to feed, bath, and dress her. It was less than dignifying for my grandmother to have, what seemed to her, total strangers changing the adult sized nappies, wipe her buttocks for her, and wash her body. All independence lost, she became at times angry, vicious, and embarrassed, a side of her I had never experienced before.

The most challenging part of it all was that there were times when my grandmother thought I was one of the home care ladies. I felt like my grandmother had forgotten who I was and the deep connection we shared. My father reassured me that she would never forget me, that it was all just a part of her illness and her passing. Even though home care had been coming to care for her for some time now, she did not know them, never remembered them from one day to the next, and absolutely hated being cared for by people she did not know. For me, this experience was indeed a blessing in disguise as it prepared me for the reality of the work I would do later, playing music at the bedside of the dying. Although I would not be required to wash or change clothing, it was the totality of the experience of walking the journey with the dying, seeing someone die, and finding comfort within the process that was important for me to learn with her. I thank her for this gift.

One afternoon, I remember sitting at my grandmother's bedside just after we had helped to change and prepare her for bed. She looked at me with a cheeky grin and whispered in a soft yet excited voice, "You know Alfie came to me last night. He told me he would come back soon to get me! And then my mother came. She is with us now and is helping me."

It reminded me of what it might be like for a prisoner to know he was going to break loose from the prison walls, my grandmother now confined to the prison of her ailing body. She seemed to glow with this notion, the formless shining through the form. Alfie was my grandmother's first husband. My grandmother did not speak of him until the final years of her life, when she chose to reveal him to me, showing photos of their wedding; she recalled their love and the tragedy of losing him so young. He died only a few weeks after they were married when hit by a car on a busy road in Sydney. The only miracle of this tragic time was that my grandmother was blessed with my aunt. After his tragic death, she learned she was pregnant with his baby, a small piece of Alfie left for her to treasure. We spoke a little longer, and then she gently closed her eyes and drifted off to sleep. I knew her love for my grandfather was great, and her wish to honor him greater, which is why I assume she did not mention Alfie before this time. The next morning, my father and I sat on the long lounge across from my grandmother's recliner. We had not thought of it before, but I just decided in the moment to pick up my flute and begin to play. Almost immediately, we noticed her fingers started to tap, her hand slowly lifting and falling to the beat. My father then gingerly picked up the guitar and began to strum the chords of Proud Mary. Upon reflection, this was the perfect song, what great lyrics to sing her out.

> *"Left a good job in the city, working for the man*
>   *every night and day*
> *But I never lost a minute of sleeping,*
> *Worrying about the way things might have been.*
> *Big wheels keep on turning,*
> *Proud Mary keeps on burning*
> *Rolling, rolling, rolling on the river."*

One thing I can say about my grandmother is that she never ever complained about her life, she lived it and accepted every moment as it was. She was a woman of God who trusted in life and its perfection, always happy, content, and loving to all whose paths she crossed. Elva Mary could certainly be proud of the life she led and was most certainly now rolling onto the great river of life. A little stream meeting the welcoming arms of the ocean.

As my father and I played music to Elva, we were both amazed at her reaction. Her head lifted from her chest and her feet began to move around to the beat. Before we knew it, she was filled with energy again, smiling and enjoying the music. It was as if the music brought her back to life.

For roughly an hour, we played music and enjoyed her for what seemed like one last hoorah, her final swan song. Not too long after we stopped the music, my grandmother again slumped in her chair, looking more deteriorated than ever. It seemed the energy it took to enjoy the music left her depleted and closer to her passing. Knowing it was time to leave, I embraced her, saying our goodbyes, both of us knowing in our hearts it would be the last time, the last goodbye. I will never forget that moment gazing deep into her fading blue eyes for the last time. My only regret was that I did not stay until her final moments to comfort and support her. She died a few days later.

As I look back on this story and this part of my life, I am deeply thankful to my grandmother for playing such a vital role in the development of my life. She always loved music and cherished our relationship. Each day I walk onto the palliative care wards I think of her, and I think of her passion for caring for others, especially when in need.

For many years of her life, Elva Mary Shrimpton devoted herself to the Legion of Mary, a group of women from her church who cared for those who were ailing and dying. They would visit them, read the Bible to them, talk with them, sit with them, and cook for them. She devoted her life to those who needed help in their last moments of life. She was the last of the Legion of Mary members to pass away, in some way passing the torch to me.

Her passing awakened that same desire to be of service, and it taught me about the reality the commission of working with the dying brings. I feel deep within my soul that it is often my grandmother who protects, guides, and supports

me when I am playing harp for patients on the palliative care
wards. Not too long before my grandmother died, she gave me
a small piece of paper she had kept in her cherished Bible for
many years. It was a prayer she spoke each day of her life and
wished to pass it onto me.

> *Make me a point of contact, Lord,*
> *Whereby the Holy Spirit may enter,*
> *Into those I touch whether by,*
> *The word I say,*
> *The prayer I pray, or*
> *The life I live.*

I had no idea of the complexity of palliative care nor the
weight of the load that family and other caregivers carry to
keep the dying wishes of their loved ones. No matter how ill
my grandmother became, she would not agree to go to hospital
and strongly resisted if my father or those caring for her tried
to force her. It was becoming more difficult to care for her by
the day, and the time for her to go to hospital was looming.
Eventually she gave in, accepting that it was too difficult to care
for her at home, and she went to hospital. I am sure my father
felt he had failed her, indeed that was not so. My father and aunt
stayed by her side for days, working in tandem so as not to leave
her to die alone.

As it turned out, she had other plans. Ironically, she died
in the silence between visits. She chose a private moment to
perhaps meet with her darling Alfie once again, take his hand,
and go home. This would not be the last time I would see this
happen. Many souls I would meet in my future work would
choose the same, simple, silent exit from this world to the next.
Certainly not the fanfare one would expect at a final farewell. I
wondered whether the fanfare was wherever they have moved
on to. We will have to wait and see.

Gary Malkin of Graceful Passages says that of all the transitions we pass through, the death of our physical body is often the most frightening, perhaps because what lies beyond is so mysterious and unknown, or is it? Is it really so unknown to us? How can it be that Elva seemed to know exactly where she was going and who would be there to meet her? Why have so many others I have sat with in their final moments had the very same experience? All these questions I am happy not knowing the answer to, though I look forward to finding out when mine is the time to see.

Healing Harps

"The playing of the harp confers a special privilege upon all harpists . . . [we have] the ability to unlock the doors of the soul."

Christina Tourin, Founder and Director of the International Harp Therapy Program

In her book, *Grace Notes, Reflections on the Harp and Healing*, Tami Briggs says, "Many people are fascinated by the harp, probably more so than any other instrument." So what is it that makes the harp so special? Apart from the fact that the harp has such a beautiful sound, it is steeped in healing tradition and loaded with symbolism that can color the way a person perceives it.

Sarah Jane Williams, an accomplished Vibroacoustic Harp Therapist and author, outlines a perspective on the history of the therapeutic harp in her book "Good Vibrations, Principles of Vibroacoustic Harp Therapy," which is particularly helpful here in exploring this subject.

Throughout the past fifty years, she says, the therapeutic effects of music upon the physiological mechanisms such as blood pressure, heart rate, respiration, metabolism, muscular energy, digestion, attention span, pain, mood, imagination, and intelligence have been well documented. Harps were often viewed as magical instruments and were played by mythical characters that possessed magical, healing, and prophetic powers. With a harp they could enchant animals and humans, lure enemies to destruction or put them to sleep, summon the seasons, and make a room tremble.

Williams goes onto say that perhaps the earliest depiction of the belief that there is magic in the plucked strings of the harp lies in a painting in the French Les Trios Frères caves (ca.15,000 B.C.) that documents a shaman playing a musical bow, an ancestor of the harp, in ritual to cast a musical spell over a bison.

Early researchers and documenters rarely distinguished between instruments such as the lyre and harp, meaning that it is possible the word harp may represents a generic class of instruments or chordophones that have at least one open string that is plucked–all of which are posed to have developed from the hunter's bow.

In its colorful history, many myths in the ancient world suggest that the harp was a celestial instrument, revered as a gift from the gods, seen as a mystic ladder and perfect communication device between heaven and earth. They were seen as talking statues, delivering messages from the gods, including one account that the Greek god of light, music, and healing, Apollo, was credited with creating the first lyre (an ancestor of the harp), by plucking the sinews on a turtle shell.

The Irish god Dagda is said to have played "three noble strains" or airs on the harp that could induce profound sleep, the release of tears, or laughter, and the earliest known records about the Druids come from Julius Caesar's accounts from third century B.C., where the bards (Druid priests or healers) held three attributes: playing the harp, knowledge of ancient lore, and poetic power.

About 2900 B.C., the Chinese literati and Buddhist monks revered the sounds of the plucked strings produced on an instrument called Ch'in. The mystical instrument was said to have the ability to heal depression, improve blood circulation, and regulate breathing. A devoted player would have good health and a long life, could achieve enlightenment, and perhaps even become immortal!

Williams's research indicates also that in the eleventh century B.C., the Judean shepherd-warrior-poet, David, soothed troubled King Saul and healed him of his "evil spirits" with song, psalms, and sweet music from his Kinnor, a common type of ancient lyre. Greek mathematician and philosopher, Pythagoras of Samos (circa 580-500 B.C.), is credited with developing the Western musical scale by calculating intervals based on the harmonic overtone series. He prescribed the use of the seven musical modes to incite or heal various emotions and preferred them to be played on the lyre. Each note of the seven-string lyre was thought to echo one of the celestial bodies (Mercury, Venus, Mars, Jupiter, Saturn, Sun and Moon).

It was Pythagoras's belief that secret symbol of the lyre was the human condition, the body of the lyre representing the physical form, the strings representing nerves and the music, the spirit. The Apollonian class of music, which used the lyre to calm and uplift the individual, was played in the Greek Asklepia or healing temples, and in 324 B.C., the sanity of Alexander the Great was said to have been restored by music of the lyre.

The ancient Romans also believed that music was curative as well as preventative, so harp music was often played following the evening meal. Because they believed the harp was a link between both worlds, it was also used as a guide through the death process. Funerary statues of harpers with their harps have been found in burial sites of the early Cycladic civilization (2800-2300 B.C.) and were found in the ancient Mesopotamian Royal Tombs of Ur.

Sarah Jane Williams concludes that in light of this aforementioned history, the archetypal associations of angels with harps, found in the Judeo-Christian traditions, might have a much deeper origin in the collective unconscious than we realize. This would definitely explain some of the reactions patients and their families have had to the harp on my visits to their deathbed rooms.

Most people I meet while working have the idea of the harp being of angelic nature, played by angels, and producing the imagined sounds of heaven. I would be a millionaire if I had a dollar for every time a person told me they thought they went to heaven while I played, or that I must be an angel because I play the harp. I promise you, when I played the flute for the ill and dying, I rarely, if ever, heard these types of comments.

For the most part, this is a positive thing, and generally people are touched by the instrument and all it seems to stand for. This is not always the case though, and many people for the very same reason, that it reminds them of heaven and angels, do not want me to play for them. One of the stories in subsequent chapters describes this very situation where a man felt it was indeed a sick joke to have a harpist in a palliative care ward playing music for the dying. Some people have even told me not to play for them for they are not ready to go yet. This is an incredibly interesting phenomenon, and it shows the power of symbolism on inanimate objects.

Maybe they fear that because of the history and symbolism surrounding the harp, it may cause them to die sooner than they desire. What I am fairly sure of is that the harp is like a mirror, reflecting back to them their situation and the reality that they are in fact dying, no matter how much they choose to deny it. It is not my intention to bring up this pain, and certainly not the harp's, but I guess after centuries of the harp being used to soothe the dying, calm ancient kings and queens, and energize gladiators and peasants, somewhere in the depths of the psyche could it be possible that our innate intelligence reminds us of the fact the harp is an instrument that can transport us to other realms? It is interesting to note that the Greek philosopher, Epictetus, said "people are not disturbed by things, but by the view which they take of them."

"Music stands before the soul without creating a picture, a name, or a form of this concrete world, and so the soul prepares itself to experience the infinite."
Hazrat Jnayat Khan

The harp is an instrument that can reach through and speak to one's soul, as reiterated by Christina Tourin, founder of the International Harp Therapy Program, who says that "playing the harp is a special privilege upon all harpists, [we have] the ability to unlock the doors of the soul." Moreover, Hal A. Lingerman, in his book *The Healing Energies of Music*, says, "Enter the list and glissando of harps and you will feel free and weightless, able to rise into lighter atmospheres and expanded feelings." Maybe this too explains things. If the harp is the type of instrument that can bring about these states of mind, body, and spirit, and there is fear of death, then the fear of allowing the harp to guide us to this place of peace is frightening. If it is true, as Don Campbell says in his book, *The Mozart Effect*, that "music is the bridge between life and death," it can be understandable that a person is scared to approach the "bridge" without anxiety and trepidation. For most of the time I feel as a healing musician it is my role to not only be the bridge but stand on the bridge. The bridge between this life and the next, using the music to, as Don Campbell says, "weave a magic carpet for the soul's journey home."

There are many and varied reasons it is believed the harp is the perfect instrument to provide an environment that is conducive to healing, and I have personally found that the characteristics of the harp are well suited to palliative care environments. The first reason I find the harp to be more suitable for playing music for the dying is because of its wide pitch range (low C to high G), which can vibrate the entire body. It also has a wide dynamic range, especially suiting those whose need requires something very soft and gentle. Early in my training, I used my first instrument, the flute, for most of my bedside sessions.

As much as this was appropriate for most people, there were many cases where the flute just did not cut it. Dynamically I felt limited, with less flexibility when needed. There were some situations where the sound of the flute was simply too much for the person, and I needed to stop. I do not seek to deter those who play flute who want to become healing musicians, nor do I wish to disregard the beauty of the flute. Although, it is important to realize our limitations and consider the environment we are working in at all times. I personally felt the harp was much better suited to palliative care due to its wide flexibility in range and dynamics, with the ability to be incredibly soft, as well as remaining expressive at all times.

This is imperative to remember when working in four-bed rooms within the ward, that there may be times when what suits one person in the room will not suit another. The more you can be aware of your environment, and be able to change your approach, the better equipped you will be for all sorts of situations. If your instrument is limiting your ability to adapt, the more difficult it may be to obtain the results you desire. The harp is a special instrument.

Tami Briggs explained that the harp has "archetypal significance as an ancient, spiritual healing instrument, which opens doors to the collective unconscious and, therefore, may facilitate the healing process."

Other attributes found by Vibroacoustic Harp Therapist Sarah Jane Williams include:

1. The historical and archetypal significance of the harp as an ancient, spiritually-healing instrument may open doors to the personal and collective consciousness, thereby facilitating the healing process.

2. It offers a varied palette of tone colors that can be soothing and calming.

3. The harp's unique ability to create an ethereal effect created through the use of enharmonic glissando.

4. When a harpist holds the harp against her body to play, it vibrates her whole body, including her electromagnetic field. Some have even theorized that playing the harp stimulates the thymus gland, the yin meridians are nourished, and the chakras, which extend several inches from the body, are actually vibrated inside the harp. (Williams, 1996)

5. The Aeolian harp may be the only instrument Mother Nature can play herself. If you have ever heard the wind play harmonics on the harp strings (which may I say I most certainly have!), you will certainly agree it's one of the most amazing and ethereal sounds ever heard. In the famous words of Henry David Thoreau: "The strains of the Aeolian harp and the wood thrush and the loftiest and truest preachers I have I know now left on this earth."

6. The muscles in our bodies resonate to harp strings and actually act like harp strings. In fact, Dr. Maria Stokes (Royal Hospital for Neuron-disability, London) found that when muscle fibers oscillate in a muscle contraction, they produce a twanging sound, heard by pressing a microphone against the skin. The thickness and length of the muscle determine the type of sound heard. (Williams, 1997)

7. The long resonance time of each note or groups of notes played on the harp allows our physiological systems to entrain more readily to the experience. (Williams, 2003)

8. The entire body is used when playing the harp, thereby stimulating more brain tissue. Williams says that changes in the brain's cortical regions, which represent somatosensory, visual, and auditory systems, have been found in musicians who play stringed instruments. These cortical regions of the brain were substantially enlarged in string players when compared to non-string instrument players through magnetic source imaging.

9. Very complex information, Williams says, can be

communicated through this simple yet elegant instrument. "No other vibrating medium (strings) except water produces such a full complement of harmonics–the wave form of a harp approximates that of the human voice. The very unique wave pattern shape is the sound equivalent of white light." *(Estes, 1998)*

Joy's Philosophy

"The Holy Spirit is our harpist and all the string which are touched in love must sound."
Met child of Magdeburg (13th Century Mystic)

I remember being so incredibly nervous, I had only been playing the harp for a short time, and I literally knew only two songs. That was it. I was panicking because I thought it would be boring and sound amateurish. As I was led into the room, Joy smiled at me, so very happy I had come to play for her. As I played she repeated, "It is so beautiful. I feel so relaxed and soothed. Thank you so much!"

Eventually, I settled into the moment, and I relaxed enough to move from this simple tune that I had practiced so hard to something I had never heard before, a song just for Joy. This would prove to be the first time I would truly enter the stillness of music and tap into something powerful. As the first simple notes entered the quiet stillness, I just knew something very different was about to happen. The sound was somehow alive with energy, conveying a manner of beauty beyond anything I had encountered previously. It seemed as if the melodies were speaking directly to her soul, revealing unexplainable truths and touching her deeply. She wept. I closed my eyes to try and absorb as much of this moment and the music as possible, time seeming to stand still.

In this moment I felt I was becoming what can only be

described as one with the music. Music so simple, yet so hauntingly beautiful it awakened a realm of experience within me I did not know was possible, especially as a so-called amateur harp player.

"One more for the road, Joy," I would say as Joy smiled and silently clapped with pleasure. I played for this lovely woman a few times, right up until her death. She even wrote me a letter telling me how much it meant to her that I played for her, calling me her angel. Even after the music had faded away gently, we sat in the silence, dwelling in such a profound awareness of the inherent wholeness of the moment. No matter how unprepared I felt I was, no matter how inexperienced, no matter how amateur, this moment was whole, and so were we. Even the stark contrast of the reality of Joy's illness that would lead to her death within days of our meeting, there was the peace that passes all understanding.

Looking back, this was to be the first of many experiences being inspired by music, now truly understanding the true evocative power that opening oneself up to the present moment could bring. A new dimension opened in my life with the thrill that the vibrations of musical sound could bring such transcendental experiences for the person, their families, and ultimately me.

I was surprised to receive a phone call from Joy's son who invited me to play for her funeral, knowing how much the music meant to her. He even sat in on one of her sessions, watching as I sat by her bed, glancing at her through the strings, her eyes closed, face glowing, and smiling the whole time. She would often say, "I don't want to go to sleep. I just don't want to miss a moment of it all." I remember the shock on her son's face the first time we met. I had been playing for Joy for quite some time, and each time she saw her family she would describe the angel with the harp who came to play for her. Her son laughed when he explained that they had all thought that it was the drugs, and that she was seeing things. "Fancy seeing an angel with a harp!" he laughed. They were all pleased I was indeed real.

The day of Joy's funeral, the family asked me to play what they liked to call a musical farewell. I picked up the harp and walked toward the dark wood casket covered with bright yellow flowers and gold fittings, perfect for such a bright person. The chair that had been prepared for me to sit in stood at the front facing the family. As I approached the chair, I felt led to make a change. I stood at the front, thanked everyone for inviting me to this very sacred occasion, and then moved forward to sit down. *No, I can't do it this way,* I thought. I looked at the floor for a moment, then the casket, then back to her son. "Would you be offended if I turned my back to you?" Completely understanding my request, her son looked at me, closed his eyes, a tear rolled down his cheek, and then he took a deep breath saying, "Definitely, it is the only way to do it."

I nodded and glanced down the line of family who were smiling and crying, thanking me with their eyes. "I had a certain relationship with Joy when I played at her bedside. It was all about her. I would like this to remain the same," I said, as I looked upon the many mourners who probably did not understand my strange request. They nodded with understanding as I picked up the chair and turned it around to face her beautifully adorned casket. I took a moment, said a silent prayer, and noticed the light shining through the stained glass window behind her. The streams of yellow light filtered down and danced in the warm walnut wood of the harp. I closed my eyes and was overjoyed to see her face again, smiling at me in anticipation. No longer did I see the casket, only the apparition of peace, just as if I were with her again.

"One more for the road," I said to myself and to Joy. I know she would have heard. I cannot tell you what I played, or for how long. All I know is that this was the first time I wept at the harp. Not because I was sad for Joy, but because I was so honored to be playing for her, music and sound weaving a magic carpet for her soul's journey home, acting as a bridge between life and death. In my mind, I saw her smiling face and swirls of what seemed like sparkling fairy dust spiraling upward toward rays of bright white light beaming through the windows. As I plucked the final string, there was a peace. It was finished.

Finally, I wiped my tear-stained face and sat in silence. The silence seemed to go on forever. Then I came to and turned around to face the crowd of people behind me. As I stood, the whole room leapt to their feet, clapping and cheering loudly. It was the most surreal experience I have ever had, especially at a funeral. They were not clapping for me; they were applauding the life of Joy.

Part-time Angel

"The end of all good music is to affect the soul."

Montiveverdi

7 made my way to begin playing, as usual, at the nurses' station. I find that spending around twenty minutes playing for the staff not only gives me the space to center myself and become attuned with the harp, but it also provides an opportunity for families and loved ones of the dying to see me and request my services.

I had barely put the harp onto my lap when a man in his mid-forties walked out from the elevators. He, like many people, circled around the nurses' station, trying hard to seem as if he were just browsing. He walked back to the elevators, stood there a moment, and then turned to find me glancing his way. Seeing he had my attention, he quickly said, "So, what do you call that?"

"Oh, hello," I said. "This is called a therapeutic lap harp."

"Is it Celtic?" he asked.

"Well, it is probably modeled on the Celtic harp somewhere along the line. This little harp has been made by a company in America, and they have built it especially for those using harp as a therapeutic tool. It is much lighter than the average lap harp, which is so very helpful when carrying the harp from room to room. It does become quite heavy!"

I carefully lifted the harp up toward him, allowing him the

opportunity to hold it and experience the feel of the instrument.

"Wow! That is light," he said with a huge grin. "Well, there you go. I have never seen a harp in the flesh before, and now I have heard one, too! That is great." He then went on to tell me that his mother was downstairs, she and his father were waiting for some tests to come back. "We have been here a couple of days, and each time we slip out for a momentary walk or cup of tea, we miss the specialist! Can you believe it?" he said with a little frustration in his voice.

"Dad and I have been playing some music for her; she likes music. It helps her, as she is a little anxious now. Actually, we all are guessing it is all the waiting that is adding to it."

"Say, do you think your mother would like some music?" I asked, sensing he might really like me to come down and play for his parents.

"Oh, that would be wonderful! Is that okay?"

"It would be my pleasure. After all, that is what I am here for."

"Really, so you come here on your own steam?"

"Yes, I am a volunteer two days per week. I play harp for the patients and their families."

"Oh, that would be lovely. I am sure that they would love it, thank you so much."

"By the way, my name is Angela."

"Lovely to meet you, Angela. My name is Roger." We proceeded to get on the elevator and travel down to the first floor where his mother and father were waiting.

"Dad, Mom, this is Angela. She plays the harp for people here at the hospital. Would you like to hear some music?"

"Oh, Patricia," his father exclaimed. "We were just saying to ourselves, harp is just what we would like to hear today, weren't we, Pat?" he said jokingly.

"Absolutely right!" she answered, going along with the joke.

"This is my father, David, and my mother, Patricia. Dad has very limited vision, but he can see colors and shapes," Roger said introducing us.

"Well, I can see that you have a lovely yellow top on, so that's great! And, I can see that your diet is doing you good as well, a lovely figure you have, don't you? I can see that much!"

We all laughed at his comments and sense of humor. "Hello, David and Patricia, it's really nice to meet you both. Thank you for the opportunity to play for you today."

"It is our pleasure I am sure!" David said with genuine excitement in his voice. "I can't wait for this." He sat down in the comfortable chair beside his wife's bed. "So, what do you do for a paid job, Angela?"

"Well, I am a musician, Kinesiologist, and writer. Lots to do!"

"And obviously you are an angel in your spare time. And with a name like Angela, there you go, it's true!" David said, his face beaming.

"Thank you! You are too kind," I said with a smile and a laugh while I prepared myself to begin to play.

"Oh, Patricia," he said to his wife who was now lying beside him. "Imagine this happening to us! Imagine having our own harpist serenading us. This is special, isn't it?"

As I began to play, I noticed David recline in his chair, his head resting back. He took off his glasses and rested them on his lap. He closed his eyes, took a deep breath, and let out a long sigh. Entering a blissful place, he sank further into the large couch. His son Roger sat in a chair across from he and his wife overlooking the whole scene with wonder and awe, obviously happy with what was unfolding.

I played with emotion and was surprised to find myself feeling quite affected by the music and the sound of the harp. I noticed David had fallen into a deep sleep, and as I glanced up through the harp strings, I found both he and Patricia resting, eyes closed and peaceful.

I completed the session as they slowly opened their eyes.

"Thank you. That was so relaxing, so beautiful," they said.

David then went on to describe when and where he met his darling Patricia. "I met her sixty-two years ago, and we have been married for sixty-one years!" he said with deep and obvious pride.

"That is amazing," I said. "What an achievement for you both."

"Yes, I met her on a blind date, would you believe? It was during the war, and I was standing on Waterloo station in London. I thought I was the king of the world standing on that platform wearing my uniform. I was much younger then, of course. Then, I looked up and saw her; I saw Patricia. I thought wow! She had long ebony black curls and a cute little green hat on that matched her green dress. And you know what? I still think wow every day," he said as he glanced at his wife with a smile and a wink.

"Gee, Patricia, he is good!" I said smiling cheekily.

"Oh my, yes, he is," she replied as her hand moved across the while sheets to find his. It was obvious how much they loved each other and how much they feared their time with each other was ending.

"You know what, Angela?" David said. "I have written in a journal every day of my whole life, and today, you will take pride of place in this journal. Thank you for all you have shared with us today. It has been very special."

I left the room feeling extremely privileged, not only for the opportunity to play music for some very warm and genuine people, but also for the pleasure of hearing their story. Simply to listen.

Most of my time is spent playing, and even though I am listening deeply to the harp, to their breath, and to the sounds of the silence in the room, I very much relish in the opportunity to put down the harp and just listen. It has reminded me of the healing effects that deep, heartfelt listening can bring.

Death Ends a Life,
Not a Relationship

*"The harp fills the atmosphere with an uplifting
transparency of sound, thus opening doors to higher
presences attending."*
H. Lingerman, *The Healing Energies of Music*

nd then there was Jill's story. Not too long after I began my work as a therapeutic musician playing harp for people who were dying, I met a woman named Jill who would challenge all I believed about what happens when we die. I had been playing for Jill for a few weeks, to start with while she was still quite bright, despite the devastating effects of cancer. Jill was a charming person surrounded by her family, staying in a room with three other women. One of the women in the room directly in front of Jill was Beth. Both women loved the music and would literally light up as I entered the room. "What would you like to hear today, ladies?" I would ask.

"Anything, anything at all. I love it all," Beth would say with genuine feeling and heartfelt expression. Therefore, I would just play, and it did not matter what I played . . . this felt freeing to me as well. After a few weeks, Jill began to deteriorate and became more ill every time I would visit. Monday morning I received a call from my supervisor, asking me to play for Jill's funeral. I felt honored to attend and play one last time for Jill and her family.

It was a sunny day, and as I drove up the driveway of the church for Jill's funeral, I was greeted by her daughter, a magnificently dressed woman with a smile that welcomed me with much love and gratitude. As I stepped out of the car, she embraced me and thanked me profoundly for coming to play for her mother. She also thanked me for all I had done for Jill in her last weeks. She then left me to prepare my harp and begin playing. I played pieces I felt Jill would have liked, and I sat by her casket remembering her and thinking of how surreal this job was. What an honor it was to be fare-welling these people at such a sacred time.

Even though the relationship with those who are dying and their families is relatively short, it seems that the lack of time encourages one to become closer to others; one is willing to cut the crap, so to speak, and get to the core of things. One is willing to be open to love and be loved by others. It is a shame we wait for such a time to do so. I often find myself saying to families that have lost loved ones in my presence that I am so very blessed to be a part of the most sacred of moments in their lives, and I find myself going home at night and appreciating my loved ones and life much more. I am grateful for their openness and for allowing me into that sacred space that is so precious to them.

The funeral ended, so I thanked the family and started to make my way out of the church. It was not until weeks later I was reminded of Jill's funeral. I came into work and made my way up to the second floor to the four-bed room where Beth was still staying. I could not wait to see how she was, if she was worse, or even alive. Most weeks I find myself preparing to walk into a room and see a different person or maybe no one at all in the bed, just a silence in the room and the realization that a friend has died. I feel a mix of disappointment and relief, then pick my harp up and move to the next room to start all over again. This particular day I walked into find Beth still there, but having deteriorated. She mustered up all her energy to turn her face toward me, smiling. "I heard all about how seamless the funeral was," she said.

"Oh, really! Yes, it was lovely. How do you know? Did you see some of Jill's family?" I asked.

"No, Jill told me!" she said with a confused look on her face. "Who do you think told me?"

I glanced at her daughter who said, "I have not seen them; I don't think Mum has either."

I turned to Beth and said, "Well, you tell Jill I was honored to have played for her funeral, and thank her for her delightful comments."

"Oh, she knows that, Angela, she knows! She told me all about the beautiful outfit you wore, black with gorgeous heels, and she loved your beads. And she told me about the music you played and how heavenly it was to hear you again."

Beth went on to describe details of the funeral, songs I played, conversations I had. The interesting thing was that she knew the names of the songs even though I never once told her what their names were. Most of the music I play is hundreds of years old, and the possibility of her knowing their names was slim. In astonishment, I stood there listening to this woman give a word for word description of the funeral and my experience of it. Moreover, there was no way she could know most of the details she described. I smiled, thanked her, and began to play as she drifted off into a deep sleep.

As I played and looked out the large glass windows that offer a pleasant view, I thought to myself that it was interesting the connections we keep, even after we die. Maybe the closer we come to death, the easier it is for us to see and hear that which by nature is unseen and unheard. Maybe I just need to listen more carefully and look more closely. There is evidence if we take the time to stop and be still.

I only played for Beth one last time about a week later. I walked in the room to find her gasping for breath, as some people do in their last moments of life. I sat beside her and played, and every now and then, she would turn to me and apologize for the gurgling noise she was making as she breathed. I smiled sympathetically and told her it was okay. She turned to me just before going off to sleep and said, "You know what? You have really improved!" People who are dying tell it like it is. I love that about them, even though sometimes this can challenge the weaker areas of my being. Working with the dying asks many things of me, most importantly to be humble and to leave my ego at the door. I am thankful to Beth for teaching me this lesson.

I sit at the bedside asking how it feels to know you are going to die any minute. I find myself asking the question, what is it like to die? How does it feel to know that your time is so very near, the cycle of life complete? Everything I ever thought about dying has been turned on its head. It seems that society can often devalue this sacred time and paint an unrealistic picture. As a result, people are scared to die, or worse, scared to live until they die. Part of settling into this job of therapeutic musician for the dying was to come to grips with the physical deterioration of the body, the lesson of seeing past the physical to see the true and pure beauty within a person's soul.

I remember feeling scared playing for the first few people who were close to death, and with time, I learned to look past this and see the miracle that is occurring before me, cherish the moment with this person and be present. The truth is, I am witnessing a simultaneous birth and death. Don Campbell, in the *Mozart Effect*, said that music acts as a bridge between life and death, and so I see myself as a type of musical midwife to the soul.

Every situation is different. Some people are in obvious pain, some are scared, some are angry, and others are at total peace. As time moves on, and with experience, I find that I can intuitively feel where the person may be on his or her journey the moment I walk in the room. I have seen people only hours before their deaths look more beautiful than any person I have ever met. They are at peace, have accepted their situation, and they radiate light. If there is such a thing as a good death, it is my hope that I may learn to die with total acceptance and peace. It seems if one can achieve this, all sorts of miracles happen in the moments leading up to the transition.

The Love in Rejection

"Sound bypasses the intellect and has the inherent ability to trigger the emotions."

Joy Gardiner Gordon,
quoted in *Vein of Gold* by **Julia Cameron**

I experienced a situation that had me fleeing, harp in hand, trying to find someplace where I could cry without others seeing me. I found myself in the garden, the sounds of the fountain and the scent of the gardenias soothing me as I sobbed. You know, it's not like I expect every bedside to be amazing . . . . or for every person I play for to like what I do.

I have had many instances where people have said no, they didn't want harp today, for whatever reason. Sometimes they just don't feel like it, or don't feel like having company, or maybe they are scared of the symbol the harp reveals. Sometimes seeing a harp brings visions of angels and heaven, which can be emotionally challenging for those who are dying, especially those who believe it is not their time. Maybe any sound can be irritating when one is sick and dying. I understand all of this and try never to take it to heart. Following is an example of when no is not necessarily a rejection.

"Oh, Angela, Brian would love the harp today. I think he plays the trombone," the nurse called. The moment I walked in the door, Brian sat up, eyes bulging from his head, staring at the harp. I introduced myself in the usual way.

59

"Hi, Brian, the nursing staff directed me to you. They thought you might like some music," I said.

"That is so fatalistic. You're not going to play me out!" he spat, appearing to be genuinely angry at the thought of even having a harpist in a palliative care ward, it seemed. Ironically enough, I must have been particularly centered that day as I found myself agreeing with him and reassuring him that it was okay by me, I certainly did not have to play for him, and yes, many people feel the same way about the harp. The strange thing was, that moments after my response, as I picked up the harp and started to leave, Brian stopped me with his hand on mine and looked up at me with very blue and subdued eyes, now filled with tears. Something had shifted for him.

"I am so sorry. I really did not mean that. Please play. I really would like to hear you play," he said with genuine feeling. Again, I let him know that it was okay, I was not offended, and that I did not need to play for him. He motioned towards the chair and pleaded with me to stay and play. So, I did. I played for around twenty minutes, and as usual, I regularly glanced over to ensure the music I was playing was agreeing with him and meeting his needs. Each and every time I looked through the vibrating strings of the harp at him I noticed he was curled in the fetal position, holding himself and staring at me with a glassy-eyed gaze. Tears flowed down his wrinkled face. There was much pain.

I finished the session and slowly lowered the harp to my lap. Brian motioned for me to come closer. I rose and braced my harp beside his bed. "Thank you for having me, Brian. It was a real pleasure to be able to play for you today," I said.

"Thank you, Angela, I loved the music, and I love you," he said, one last glistening tear gliding down his face.

The harp has been used as a "healing" instrument for as long as history has been recorded, and likely well before that. The historical and archetypal significance of the harp as an ancient, spiritually healing instrument opens many doors to the personal and collective unconscious. In the ancient world, the harp was universally revered as a gift from the gods; it was a mystic ladder and perfect communication device that connected heaven and earth. In 324 B.C., the sanity of Alexander the Great was said to have been restored by music of the lyre, an early form of the harp. The ancient Romans also believed that music was curative as well as preventative, so harp music was played following the evening meal. *(McClellan, 1988)*

Because the harp was seen as a link between both worlds, it was also used as a guide through the death process. How interesting that we find ourselves thinking we are pioneers in a craft! Funerary statues of harpers with their harps have been found in burial sites of the Early Cycladic civilization (2800-2300 B.C.), while the remains of actual harps and their harpers (2700 B.C.) were found in the ancient Mesopotamian Royal Tombs of Ur. Thank God, I am playing for the dying in the twenty-first century! In knowing this history, I can understand it is possible that when Brian saw the harp he reacted to what the harp meant to him. Maybe the harp reminded him of angels and heaven … and dying. The harp may have acted as a mirror for his condition as well as his situation.

As challenging as this situation was, it was nothing compared to what I experienced only days later. I was asked by a nurse to try and help a lady relax. She was very anxious, breathing heavily, and obviously in a lot of pain. It just so happened that this lady was sharing a room with three others. I walked in behind the nurse, she introduced me to the patient, and all in the room seemed delighted to have me there. One lady was unconscious, one I knew and she smiled warmly, the other I did not think I had met before, though she seemed excited to see and hear the harp.

I began the session, focusing on the lady for whom I had been sent in to play. Slowly, she began to respond, her breath slowing, her moaning decreased, and she began to settle. Her son walked over to the drawer beside her bed and took out the Vicks Vapor rub. He sat at her feet and rubbed them, and I could smell that familiar scent of eucalyptus in the air. It is such a comforting scent, reminding me of my childhood, having my mother gently rub it on my chest when sick with colds and flu.

I had been playing for a while, when the woman diagonally across from us called out, "Can't you play something different? Play something different for God's sake; it's the same old thing over and over and over again. It is so boring!"

A little shocked, and most certainly slightly put off, I glanced her way saying, "You know, I completely understand that not everybody likes the same music. I will be finished in a few moments."

"Well, I don't know. What does everyone else think? Don't you think that it is incredibly boring? Don't you wish she would play something else?"

Torn between meeting the needs of my client and being very aware of the irritated woman in the bed across the room, I was understandably uncomfortable. I had not come across this situation in such a magnified way before. I continued to play something I thought was a bit different, when I began to hear her speaking under her breath again, this time with what could only be described as seething anger. I glanced over toward her again, and I noticed that her face was getting redder by the minute as she repeated the words, "You're torturing me, you're torturing me, and you can't even play something just for me!"

By this time, I too was becoming emotionally overwhelmed so I completed the session, fought back the tears forming in my eyes, and thanked the patient and her son. He smiled at me, looking a little uncomfortable himself. As I walked out, head down and heart aching, the little lady I knew called out, "Thank you, Angela!" I gave her a shy smile and kept walking.

I walked out of that room, no, I almost ran out. In hindsight, it seems ridiculous. I went straight for the elevators, trying to find the easiest way out of the building, out into some fresh air and a place to let go. As I sat in the garden outside, tears rolling down my face, I remember promising myself I would never do this again! However, one cannot ignore the inner prompting of the soul, the passion of purpose, and the drive to overcome and succeed. With the passing of time, and much support from those who have walked this path before me, I sit here writing my story coming to peace with what happened. I have decided to not allow one experience taint the rest of the beautiful experiences I have had. I have played for hundreds of patients, and most were beautiful indeed.

Therese Schroder explains that it is the job of the musician to set up the physical conditions in which one can enter into depths of the entire process of dying. At our best we can help to transform the palliative care unit into a sanctuary for life's completion. Excellent palliative care is not about prettifying death. It takes a great deal of courage for a therapeutic musician to accompany a patient during the liminal phase of dying, as well as during that final mile home. It was not until this time I completely understood what she meant by that and how truth filled these words were.

For months after this experience, I literally lost my nerve. Prior to this, I found it incredibly easy to walk into patients' rooms and ask whether they would like music, and without a second thought I would stay and play or leave depending on what their needs were. It really did not bother me when people said no, until that point, that is. Suddenly, I found myself shrinking and feeling huge amounts of fear at the thought of entering a patient's room. If there was any indication the patients did not want me there, I would almost run. Something needed to change. Either I got over this and grew, or I stopped doing this work for good. I had to make a choice.

I remember sitting at home one day, anxiety ridden about

the whole experience and wondering what I should do. It was then I glanced over at an old table given to my husband and me by some friends of ours. The table belonged to a beautiful couple who have since passed away. They were incredibly loving and spiritual and I often look over and feel thankful that we have some of their furniture to remind us of them. I stood up and walked over to the table deciding I would look inside the drawer. I slid open the drawer and looked inside to find an article I did not remember seeing before.

It was a copy of an interview: *The Quest for Wholeness, Elisabeth Kübler-Ross.* (Written by Samantha Trenoweth.) I picked it up from the dusty drawer and walked back to the lounge chair to read it. *Kübler-Ross* was one of the most well respected researchers of life after death, death, and dying. To this end, she travelled the globe for fifty weeks of the year, lecturing in halls, visiting patients, and holding workshops to aid in the release of people's negativities, and banishing fears of death with a contagious love of life. I have read most of her books, but something in this article changed the way I looked at my work forever. The interviewer asked Kübler-Ross whether she had ever felt like she had reached the end of her tether. Her answer made my heart stand still; it felt as if Elisabeth was speaking to me in that moment.

"Until a few years ago there were many times that I was ready to quit but always, when you're at the end of the rope, something, it can be something very small but always something very significant happens. Then you make it through another day. At the beginning of my work with dying patients, I existed that way every single day. They would spit in my face in the hallway of the university hospital. I think that's where I learned that other people's opinion of you is literally their problem because the bigger the resistance or the hate, or the resentment, the more it gave me fuel to continue this work because it was a reflection of how much fear they had."

During her life's work, she had been called a vulture and a saint; she had been spat at and awarded honors. In addition, she gave us the opportunity to re-examine our attitudes towards death. Suddenly, I see. I can feel her with me, and I understand the nature of the work I am doing. Changing my focus, I now look upon the order of service of a dear lady who had passed earlier in the year. I rest my eyes upon her contribution to its content.

"Life is so terribly short, take everything in, enjoy everything, even a dull day can be beautiful. Make use of all of your life, be happy, make other people happy, forget upsets, and don't waste a minute of it."

Forget upsets? And so, yes, I will (and did) go back. I will take up my courage and keep walking forward. I will remain faithful, harp in hand, to a call that began in purity, unexpectedly and without fanfare. Counting my blessings, I am sure the harpists who were found in the Mesopotamian Royal Tombs of Ur in 2700 B.C. needed courage far greater than mine! And what courage it would have been. That same courage in a long tradition of therapeutic musicians, I can now gather into myself. I think of the courage that Elisabeth Kübler-Ross needed to complete her life's work, work that has changed the world and its view of death and dying.

The Gift of Balloons

"Music washes away from the soul the dust of everyday life."

Red Auerbach

Sometimes I am lucky enough to journey with a person for a little while, having the chance to get to know him or her more deeply, and share his or her experience more fully. This is the story of a unique woman who allowed me into her life on the final mile home, and she showed me the gift of laughter even when facing incredible pain and suffering.

We will call her Marge. Marge was a young woman who seemed to be extremely accepting of her situation as to having cancer and dying. She had been asking the staff and other volunteers to pass on the message that she would love to hear me play harp for her for many weeks, but unfortunately, at that time I was away and received the message much later.

This was the very first time I would meet Marge, and little did I know this would be such a special and unique experience for all of us. I walked into the room to find a very frail, auburn-haired woman, sitting up in bed surrounded by family and friends. They sat by her bedside talking with her and rubbing cream into her dry arms and legs. As soon as I walked in the door, Marge sat up and said, "Oh boy, finally you have come!" She seemed to be extremely excited that I had made my way to her at last. The first thing I noticed as I walked in was the huge bunch of colorful balloons that adorned the room, along with flowers and cards, not the usual scene in a palliative care ward. Flowers, yes, but a room filled with a rainbow of balloons, no.

"Yes, I am sorry. I have been away, but as soon as I heard the message you wanted to hear the harp, I came straight here!" I explained apologetically. In this case, I was lucky as there are many times I miss people, whether they die or go home, sometimes the fact that I am only in on one or two days means that by the time I go back onto the ward time has run out. I guess I just have to trust that all is perfect and do my best to get to the ones I can. Marge smiled warmly as I set up the harp on my lap; she moved her pillows around behind her as if preparing for something very special.

As I looked around the room I said, "Wow, Marge, the balloons are beautiful. Every color in the rainbow! What is the celebration?"

"It is my birthday!" she shared as she simply beamed.

"Oh, that is lovely. Happy Birthday, Marge. I am so pleased to be able to play for you on your birthday!"

"Me, too, what a lovely end to a wonderful day," she said, everyone around her smiling, trying with all their might to hide the tears forming in their eyes with the sadness of the overall situation. The odds were that this would be her last birthday. She finished her preparations and then closed her eyes, ready and waiting for me to start. I began to play. Nothing extraordinary, just soothing, soft, and relaxing music that literally put Marge to sleep in what seemed like minutes. Likewise, I noticed the people around her beginning to fall asleep, the telltale head nods showing all the signs that they too were resting peacefully. Even I felt especially relaxed during this session and found myself sitting back in my chair, caressing the harp as the delicate rays of the sun filtered through the partially drawn curtains as they flapped in the breeze. You could hear a pin drop.

All of a sudden, without any warning, one of the colorful

balloons above Marge's bed burst with a huge BANG! The after affects were something to behold as we all firstly jumped at least ten feet in the air, screamed at the tops of our lungs, and then, after a huge sigh of relief began to laugh hysterically, tears of relief running down our faces. It was simultaneously the funniest and saddest thing I have ever witnessed in my life. Only moments before we were in a state of complete relaxation. Marge and her family were actually sleeping, she in her bed, and they in their chairs when the blast woke us with a start.

For the next few minutes we laughed and laughed until tears rolled down our red cheeks. We laughed because of the looks on our faces and the amazing possibility that it would even happen. It was so healing. At one point, Marge said trying to catch her breath between giggles, "That scared the life out of me!" Then she burst into fits of laughter again, realizing what she had said. Her sister looked sideways, holding her mouth, not knowing whether to laugh as well or not. Eventually everyone joined in laughing with her. Marge would nod, trying to find her breath, and wipe the tears that were literally streaming down her face. What sort of sick joke could that be, I thought to myself? We were all so shocked at her amazing ability to see the funny side of things, even at this moment. Everyone around her thought it was absurd, yet so very beautiful that she could see the humor in the fact the she was dying, and yes, the bang scared the life out of her. Indeed, it scared the life out of me!

After this strange event, I had Buckley's chance of anyone relaxing again, so we all talked for a moment or two, and I then packed up and left, promising to come back soon and play for her again. She was thankful, and she smiled as I left.

About a week later, I popped my head into Marge's room to find her looking a little frustrated and upset. She had severe bleeding from her mouth and gums, and she seemed overwhelmed. At times, it is difficult to look beyond the physical side of the deterioration of someone with cancer, but with a person such as this, her beautiful light and spirit shone through the pain and suffering to penetrate my heart. Not everyone experiences the same thing, not everyone suffers the way others do, and it is hard to say why. All I know is that some people have the ability to transcend the pain and limitations teaching us all how to live more fully in the moment, essentially living and giving until they die.

I immediately put down my harp and asked her if she needed any help. Smiling awkwardly she pointed towards the tissue box on the table and asked if I would bring them to her. I walked over to the table and lifted them up, gently handing them to her. She did what she had to do with the tissues, and then she settled back down into her bed. I sat down to begin as she closed her eyes, again ready to relax, this time knowing the serenity would not be broken, as the colorful balloons were now only a memory and no longer in the room. The room looked so different without their vibrancy to enhance it. I played for a while as she slept, and I noticed that at various times, as she became more relaxed that her body would jerk involuntarily, at one time she jolted around so violently that she woke herself up. Eventually the spasms became mere twitches, and slowly her body relaxed fully and became still. When I finally crept out of her room at the completion of the session, she slept soundly and peacefully.

The last day I saw Marge, I entered to find her asleep, and she had deteriorated. Her family welcomed me saying that it was nearly her time and that she was sleeping almost all of the time now. She was again surrounded by family and loved ones, and they all felt sure that Marge would insist that I play for her again. One family member turned to me and said, "Do you think she will hear you, Angela?"

"I am certain she will. It is said that our hearing is the very last sense to go as we die," I whispered with tears forming in my eyes. I played soothing music that would hopefully relax and bring peace, not only to Marge, who was quite peaceful now, but more so to the grieving family surrounding her bed. There comes a time in the journey with a patient when the focus often shifts from him or her to the people around the patient. There seems to be a point where patients are neither here nor there, making their way across the bridge of life. It is at this time I get the feeling that in many cases the suffering has ended, and the time of peace has begun for that person. It is also at this time when another journey for the family and friends left behind begins, and the process of letting go waits.

After a while, I stopped playing, and as I did, Marge woke looking incredibly disorientated. One of the elderly women at her bedside said, "She knows you have stopped playing. Can you continue?"

I played for another fifteen minutes or so; all the while Marge groaned and sighed along with the music, sometimes in perfect pitch. After a while, her breathing became inaudible, the family wondering if she was actually still here. As I played the very last note, the same elderly woman turned to me and smiled. She nodded as if to say–That is it, well done, it is finished.

A few days later, I was walking through the ward when I noticed Marge's empty room. It was a strange feeling when I realized after doing a double take that she had gone. I know they are dying, but this awareness never changes the feeling when it becomes a reality. I stopped in the hallway to remember Marge and the lesson she taught me of the importance and power of laugher in the midst of pain and fear of our impending death. I closed my eyes for just a moment and imagined the room filled with rainbow hued balloons and the smile of the auburn-haired woman. The bed sheets where stark white, it was empty and bare, the windows open wide. I noticed the beauty of the curtains dancing in the breeze. She was home; a new journey had begun for us both.

There is a Rainbow over the River

"Each night when I go to sleep, I die. And the next morning, when I wake up, I am reborn."

Mahatma Gandhi

This is a beautiful story of a little old man who seemed to touch the heart of all who met him. I will call him Peter. On the day I first met Peter I felt led to sit in one of the sunny waiting rooms on the ward. The sun streaming through the large hospital windows warmed my back on a cold day. It did not take long before a young woman walked out of one of the adjacent rooms searching for the sounds of the harp that often float down the hallways and drift into patient rooms.

After following her senses, she found me sitting in the sun-filled room. She smiled and walked towards me. Her father had heard the music and begged her to go and find where the music was coming from. Very respectfully, she asked if I might possibly be willing to come and play for her father. Of course I was. She clapped her hands with joy and immediately asked what she could do to help me get my harp and myself into his room. So very excited her hands thrust outward to the harp, and without a thought, I handed her the instrument. She beamed as she turned around and walked back towards her father to give him the good news.

We walked in to Peter's room, his daughter leading the way

71

and presenting the harp to him with such enthusiasm.

"Look who I found, Dad! This is Angela, and she is going to play the harp for you. What do you think about that?"

"Oh, thank you, thank you. That is so lovely, thank you," he said.

"It is my pleasure. What is your name?" I asked as I began to sit down beside him.

"Peter, my name is Peter."

"Nice to meet you, Peter, I hope you like the music," I said. Peter was a tiny man with little grey wisps of hair upon his head. Even though he looked extremely ill, his smiled filled the room with joy, and he was a pleasure to meet. I began to play, and within moments, Peter's hands lifted in front of him, his thin arms holding them up. At first, I was not sure what he was doing, and then it became clear. His elderly fingers moved in time with the music, he watched my hands and mimicked the movements, his fingers plucking the air, sweeping the imaginary strings. He then closed his eyes and rested his hands on his lap, a smile on his face. At the completion of this session, there was stillness in the room. Peter opened his eyes, and with a tear rolling down his cheek, he thanked me for the beautiful music.

A few days later, I came back to the room to visit him again. Peter was sharing his room with four other men, all gentle people who were happy to have music brighten their day. I walked up the hall and peeped around the corner room to see whether Peter was still there. As soon as he saw my face, he smiled and glanced to my hands to see whether I had the harp. I did and his smile broadened. I searched around the room for a chair to sit in and as I did, I looked out of the large windows that framed dark rumbling clouds that threatened a storm. Then little by little, a rainbow of bright colors began to appear, spreading like a paintbrush across the sky. It spanned across the entire window and became brighter with every moment that passed by. I made my way to Peter's bedside and implored to him look at the beautiful rainbow outside!

"Oh, it is beautiful" he said, and then he began to sing. He sung gently, but with such joy, the words of song I had never heard before.

"There's a rainbow over the river, the skies are clearing, and you'll soon be hearing a heavenly song all the day long."

He repeated the chorus until I could barely hear him as he drifted off to sleep. Much of the lyric I did not quite hear.

"He loves that song," said his wife. "He always has."

I told myself I would find out the rest of the words. Even some of the older patients in the room did not know the song as it was so old. I sat with Peter for a while longer, the room was silent, and we all stared out the window at the massive rainbow in front of us until it slowly disappeared again.

A woman who was sitting with her dying sister in the room across the way appeared behind us and complimented me on the music. It broke the stillness and prompted me to ask whether she thought her sister might like some music, too. She was delighted, so off we went. I had noticed this woman at the hospital many times. Day or night, she stood by her sister's side.

I had a strange feeling the next time I saw Peter would be my last, and as it turned out, I was right. I came onto the ward in the usual way. I peeked around the corner of the room to find Peter's bed empty. I stood staring out the window that once held the beautiful rainbow wondering whether he had died or been moved. A familiar voice came from behind me; it was the woman from the room across the hall.

"He has gone downhill," she said. "I can show you where he is. Come with me," she beckoned.

"How is your sister?" I asked.

"She is strong," she said. "She is my baby sister, and she is hanging on for some reason."

"You have been here for a long time, haven't you?" I asked.

"Yes, this is my home away from home. I only leave her for a short time if I need to run errands and such. Apart from that, I stay here with her day and night. I sleep here as well. I will not leave her. You know what, though? We are all one big family here. We all know what we are each going through deeply, the pain and frustration of watching our loved ones slip away before our very eyes. This place is a sanctuary, a place to be, where all understand our pain. A glance, a smile, a look, or a touch is all it takes from another in this place and we know. Most times we do not need to speak for there are no words really." She looked at me with focused eyes. "This is where I am meant to be right now. It is my honor to walk with thee."

She smiled and pointed the way to Peter's room. I thanked her for her kindness, and then I turned to Peter's door. Just before I proceeded, I glanced back for a moment. The woman had returned to her seat in the sun beside her dying sister. She picked up her book, a romance novel, I could tell by the cover. Her short, silver hair glistened in the sun. It occurred to me that this would be the last time I would see this vigilant woman pacing the hallways of the hospital or standing by her loved one's bedside. The time was drawing near. The next day I would visit her sister's room to find it empty. The chair occupied for so many weeks would sit in the sun without the special grey-haired lady. Her baby sister would finally let go. I said my goodbyes in that moment, and I was thankful.

I turned back and knocked on the door very softly. I slowly pulled the drawn curtain back to reveal Peter's wife standing at his bedside. When she realized it was me she smiled and instantly stood up and put a chair at Peter's bedside for me to sit on. Without too much fuss, she thanked me for coming and said how much he enjoyed the music and loved my visits. The room was dark, the curtains were drawn, and no possibility of seeing a rainbow today I thought to myself.

Peter's fragile body lay underneath the crisp white sheets of the hospital bed, his bony knees kept warm by a multicolored hand-knitted blanket. The color had left his face and his eyes seemed glazed over and grey, life draining from his body like the sands in an hourglass. Time was of the essence. Time was growing short. His devoted wife reached out for his pale hand and grasped it tightly.

"Peter, dear," she said in a loud voice. "Angela is here to play music for you. Isn't that wonderful?" Peter had deteriorated very much and could only manage a slight tilt of his head to look at me. He stared blankly for a moment, and then a smile crept onto his ailing face, a smile that brightened the darkened room. He clapped his hands lightly and settled back down to rest. Generally, his wife had always been quiet while I played. She sat at his side and knitted. Even when I had finished, she was for the most part unresponsive. Peter did most of the talking, or singing. She sat in the chair beside him knitting as usual.

"What are you knitting?" I asked while setting the harp on my lap.

"A purple rug to keep Peter's knees warm," she said glancing at him with a worried look on her face. "You know what, though? I fear he will not give me the time to finish it," she said with a tear in her eye. I realized in that moment why every time I saw her she was knitting; she was racing against the clock, the sands in the hourglass were draining faster than her needles could move. She looked down again and kept knitting.

I began to play music, and only moments after, she stopped and picked up the woolen purple rug and needles, placed them on the floor beside her, and proceeded to lean on the lifted bedrail on Peter's bed. Staring into space for a time she then laid her head on her folded hands and began to silently weep. She lay there for the longest time as I played. I felt helpless and honored at the same time.

Through the stillness, a small voice spoke. There is nothing you can do. Just be brave enough to stay, and be in this moment, a snapshot of time, of witnessing another human being experiencing the all-encompassing grief we all dread. She sat upright and dried her eyes with her rose-covered handkerchief. Yellow roses, my grandmother's favorite, I thought to myself. "You know, we have been married for sixty-two years," she said with pride in her faltering voice. I sat and listened. Words would not form in my clumsy mouth, yet my hands played music with ease, a tear rolled down my face.

"It is so hard! It is so hard to watch him die. To sit here and watch him die!" she said with tears streaming down her face. "There is nothing I can do, nothing I can do to help him, nothing I can do to keep him here. He is slipping away from me; I am losing him more and more by the minute." Her voice was full of desperation as she gasped for air. I sat quietly. The silence was piercing.

"What do you do to get through this?" I whispered.

"I just do normal things. I pay the bills. I do the ironing, although these days there is less and less ironing now that Peter is going. I cook and I clean. I go to the butcher to buy meat for our dog. I think I will need to find the dog another home as he is far too big for me to take care of, and when Peter goes I will have to sell the house. I will then move into something smaller as our large house is far too big for me to care for now. So much is changing so fast."

"How long have you had your dog?" I asked.

"Nine years. He is part of the family, so it will be hard." A long pause hung in the air. "Do you think Peter knows I am here? Do you think he really knows?"

"Yes," I assured. "You know, I have played for hundreds of patients and every now and then you get a very special person. Peter is one of those people. Thank you for allowing me to get to know him and spend time with him. Thank you for allowing me to share this moment with you."

"Thank you," she said. "You know he loved your music. Did you hear all the words to the song he was singing for you the other day, the rainbow song?"

"Yes, I remember it, but I could not really hear the words very well."

"Well, he was singing a special song for you. Your music helped him very much, you know."

"Do you think you could share the rest of the song with me?" I asked tentatively.

"Sure," she said and began to relay the words to the song Peter had sung to me that wonderful moment when the rainbow appeared in his room only days ago.

"Clouds over me form a white tapestry; skies untoward are blending, winds dying down.
It's so peaceful around, now that the storm is ending.
See what nature's handiwork has done, after every shower comes the sun
There is a rainbow over the river, the skies are clearing
You'll soon be hearing a heavenly song, all the day long
Let's you and I go sailing, along the rippling stream
Holding hands together, together we will dream
With a rainbow on the river, you get the feeling romance is stealing
Right out of the blue, into your heart
There is a rainbow over the river
The skies are clearing
You'll soon be hearing a heavenly song
All the day long."

Jamie Redfern

He knew exactly what was coming, I thought to myself as tears rolled down my face at hearing the words to this beautiful song. I left Peter's room that day with a heavy heart, indeed.

Later that day, I looked out over a beautiful river. I sat in a coffee shop admiring the river and backdrop of mountains, a lovely sight, and thought about Peter as I wrote in my journal about the experience. As I thought about Peter and how much he had touched my heart, I looked up to see before my eyes a beautiful sunset, but it was more than that. As I focused my eyes I noticed a brilliant glowing ball of light in the sky, the clouds drifting above. As I looked at them, a rainbow of color appeared. I could not believe it. There was a rainbow of colors in the sky, a rainbow over the river. Was this a message from Peter? Who really knows, but I'd like to think so. The rainbow faded in a moment of time and the brilliant light eased behind the darkening clouds.

I found out the next morning when I returned to visit Peter that he had passed away peacefully in the late afternoon a few hours after I left him.

"Let's you and I go sailing, along the rippling stream holding hands together; together we will dream."

Goodbye for now, Peter, peaceful travels.

The Silence
Between Breaths

"After silence that which comes nearest to expressing the inexpressible is music."

A. Huxley

he called my name from across the hall, almost as if she was out of breath.

"I have been looking for you all over, Angela! Do you think you could come downstairs and play for a friend of mine who is dying? Her name is Annie. She is still so young, and her family is devastated. My mother told Annie's family how much she loved the harp, and they have asked me to come and find you."

"Yes, of course! Do you want me to come now?" I said, harp in hand and ready.

"Actually, yes, if you don't mind. It would be better if you came now, as her time is short."

"Lead the way," I said, following her down the hall and into the elevator.

We walked to find a room filled with grieving family. As I made my way in, their faces lit up with smiles shadowed with pain. It was obvious they were happy to see I had arrived in time, but in moments like these, it is difficult to reveal one's true joy.

"Hi, my name is Angela, and I am a volunteer here," I

whispered. In this case, I felt it was important to explain to everyone present exactly what I intended to do, and as I had anticipated, the family was happy to allow me to try various musical techniques to help Annie relax.

"Do you mind if I pull up a chair closer to Annie?" I asked.

"No, please do," the family replied. Instantly, they shuffled and moved around, until there was room beside her bed for me to place my chair. I lifted the harp above the heads of the grieving people surrounding her and sat down in the space provided.

"Do you mind if I speak to her?" I queried in a gentle tone.

"That's fine," her husband said, a single tear staining his cheek. His eyes were red and swollen from many tears he had cried in the lead up to this moment. I closed my eyes, centered myself, and then leaned forward to speak to Annie. "Hi, Annie" I said softly. "My name is Angela. I am going to play some music for you on the harp. Just relax. It's okay to go to sleep, we will not mind at all. I hope you like the music."

I gently placed my hand on hers and gave her husband a glance to let him know I would now begin. He nodded and smiled as best he could. Annie was breathing anxiously, her hands clasped the starchy white sheets, and her face appeared fearful. Her breath was heavy, labored and fast, with little or no room for relaxation or rest. Her time was indeed near, yet it seemed she was hanging on, so to speak, for some reason. Her husband stood by her side holding her hand and stroking her arm, while her sister lightly brushed the hair back from her face and caressed her pale cheek.

I watched Annie closely, the rhythm of her breath and the rise and fall of her chest. Her breath was still very heavy as I focused on matching the rhythm of the music to it. Once I felt that we were in harmony with each other, I began to slow down the music with the hope that Annie would follow. To my surprise and joy, she did follow me, and I noticed her hands, once white with tension, began to loosen and release the sheets.

Her arms relaxed and her breathing continued to slow down and became less anxious. Eventually, I began to play music without meter, which brought a deep peaceful silence to the room. Now Annie's breath was so soft we could barely hear it, some wondering if she was breathing at all.

I took a deep breath and continued to play music that was soothing and un-metered, hoping to allow Annie to fully relax and let go. Non-rhythmic music replicates the sounds of nature, the ebb and flow of the ocean waves, songbirds in flight, and the wind dancing with dried leaves in the autumn.

Many people ask why I prefer to play music that is non-rhythmic when someone is close to death. In my experience, and the experience of many other therapeutic musicians, known music has the ability to anchor or ground a person. If the person who is dying hears music that he knows, or music that is attached to a memory or experience, he is more likely to become interested and focused on this music, which prevents the gradual disengage from this life. Sometimes called sedative, the sound of non-rhythmic music can also be effective in helping to transcend pain and calm anxiety.

There is no hard and fast rule with this, and every person is different. The most important aspect for me as a therapeutic musician is to remain open to all the possibilities of what each person may need in any given circumstance. This type of therapeutic music is unique in that I can monitor the patient and change the music to meet patients' immediate needs in every moment. Not everything works every time, and so I need to be open to following the lead of the patient and listening to my inner guidance.

The look on the faces of the family surrounding Annie was priceless as they too noticed her breath slowing and easing. Her sister whispered, "She is relaxing, she is settling down . . . Look! She loves the music, doesn't she?"

She picked up Annie's hand and caressed it against her

cheek saying, "Her hand is becoming cold." She glanced up at Annie's husband who was crying silent tears that ran down his face as he took Annie's hand between his and rubbed it to try to warm her cooling skin.

With each passing moment, Annie's breath became slower to the point where her sister was softly counting the seconds between her deep breaths. Everybody looked on with hesitant excitement and interest, fascinated with all that was taking place before them. I too was deeply fascinated and could not believe the power the music seemed to have. Eventually, Annie's sister was counting up to twenty seconds between each breath.

The silence was deafening as everybody waited anxiously to see if this breath would be Annie's last. "I think she is gone," her sister whispered, a tear flowing down her cheek. Suddenly, Annie would breathe again and startle everybody present. At first, all would sigh with relief, but as this continued it seemed that they genuinely wished rest for her, and they seemed disappointed as she drew yet another deep breath. I continued to play music that ebbed and flowed, riding on the waves of Annie's final breaths.

I played for what seemed like quite some time, occasionally glancing her way to watch her chest, wait for her response and follow her lead. Finally, I looked up and noticed she was very still, and her chest did not move. In that moment, we all knew Annie was gone. You could hear a pin drop in the room as we paused to take in the magnitude and gift of the moment before us.

We turned to notice a young man, her brother, standing behind us in the doorway, stunned at the vision before him. Was she waiting for him? I wondered. For the longest time nobody moved, partly in shock, and partly engaged in the peace that filled the room. I had done all I could do for Annie. It was time to step back and allow the family their last moments with her. I stood and thanked them without breaking the silence and fumbling with speech. "Thank you for allowing me the honor of playing for Annie and inviting me into this moment." With an unspoken understanding, they thanked me with tearful smiles, and I picked up the harp and walked out into the corridor. What a privilege and honor to have served not only Annie, but also her grieving family at this most sacred time of life.

This experience brought to mind a phrase I once read in a special book called Tuesdays with Morrie. Morrie, a dying man, proffers to his young friend, "It's good to count your breaths now and then, it keeps you putting things off." Time for Annie was down to the moments left between each breath. How many of us realize we are all on this same path, never truly knowing when our last breath will be drawn.

"Everybody knows they are going to die, but nobody believes it," Morrie continues. "If we did, we would do things differently. There is a better approach. To know you are going to die and to be prepared for it any time. That way you can be more involved in your life, while you're living it."

Upon hearing this, we wonder what we can do to be better prepared for our time. Thankfully, Morrie, who is in the midst of his passing, gives us a clue by explaining what the Buddhists do to prepare themselves for death.

"Do what the Buddhists do," Morrie suggests. "Every day have a little bird on your shoulder that asks, 'Is today the day? Am I ready? Am I doing what I need to do? Am I being the person I want to be?' The truth is, if you really listen to that bird on your shoulder, if you accept that you can die at any time, then you might not be as ambitious as you are.

"The things you spend so much time on, all this work you do, might not seem as important. You might have to make room for some more spiritual things."

I take a sober moment to absorb this moment and all that it has taught me.

Everyone, every situation, and every death is different. Some people die in the silent moments when left alone, and others wait, hanging on, using every bit of energy they have to hang on until their beloved has arrived. I guess it depends on the person, their needs, and their acceptance of death itself.

I have observed, as have others, that the perceptions of the grieving family play a vital role, and they may influence the way in which someone experiences death. I believe that the more we can accept the flow of the cycles of life, and embrace challenges, the easier and more peaceful it will be for us to die.

I believe this to be true because I see the effects of resistance to death each time I enter the palliative care ward. Masaru Emoto depicts this concept of moving with the flow of life perfectly in his awe-inspiring book *The Secret Life of Water*. He opines that the act of living is the act of flowing. If a dam is built in a river to stop its flow, the river will die. Likewise, if the flow of blood gets dammed up in our bodies, somewhere it will mean the end of life.

This concept can be translated to all areas of life including spiritual, emotional, and physical. If we continue to resist the flow, allow our feelings to build up within our bodies, and resist change, then we face the probability that illness and unease will fill our being.

There seems to be an unwritten law that *when we resist, that which we resist persists.* Do people wait to die until the quiet moments of the night when family have left because the connection and love they share is so strong that it prevents them from letting go? Does this bond hold us here? Is it because they want to protect those they are leaving behind? I guess we will not know until we face it for ourselves, the one experience we are all preparing for, our own passing, and journey to a life beyond. The one experience we must do alone.

The Unseen
and Unheard

"Don't play what's there, play what's not there."

Miles Davis

I remember a lovely session with a very elderly woman I had played for a few times before. This woman was in and out of consciousness and close to her time to move on. She did, though, seem comfortable and at peace. As I walked in, her daughter introduced me, and the lady said, "I know Angela, we are already good friends!"

"Yes, of course we are. Would you like some music today?" I asked.

"Oh yes, please," she said weakly.

I sat down next to her and started to play, when all of a sudden, the woman turned to look straight in front of her. She smiled and said warmly, "Oh yes, I remember you!"

She glowed as she began a lengthy conversation with someone neither her daughter nor I could see. It was as if I was playing music for a movie scene, lifting, shaping, defining the music as she spoke so lovingly to the unseen. Her daughter put her hand on my shoulder and said, "I am sorry. I have never seen her do this before. Are you okay with this?"

"Oh, yes," I said, "most definitely. She is in a very good place. It is okay." The conversation went on for what seemed like an eternity.

85

"Oh, wouldn't it be nice to go to this music? . . . Oh, okay, I understand it is not time. . . . Oh, yes, I understand. Thank you. I love you." She would speak, and then there would be silence as she nodded and listened to the replies of the unseen and unheard, and then she fell into a deep sleep. I turned to find her daughter crying into her hands. Apparently, she died not too long after that. I love how this job takes me to places that challenge everything I ever thought about death, and most of all, about living.

These sorts of experiences happen on a regular basis, with many of the patients I play for being very close to their time to die, moving in and out of consciousness and speaking to people who the families will confirm have already passed. Some families are comforted by this expression of the dying, and others are troubled. I have noticed during the many bedside serenades that as people enter the final stages of the process of their dying that the eyes seem to grow dim and somewhat grey.

But what is more interesting is that it seems that the more the physical sense of sight diminishes, the more the patient seems to see more of what is unseen. I cannot say for sure that what they are seeing is real, all I know is that for the patient, it becomes their reality, and a peace for many. For those who seem fearful of their deaths, seeing a passed on family member brings peace of mind before the transition, and the promise that all will indeed be okay.

Many patients have confided in me, telling me their husband, mother, father, or even Jesus has come to them, and often they have been told they will be back to get them soon. Even my own beloved grandmother expressed that her first husband Alfie was with her, along with her mother, and that they promised to come for her.

I now find it hard to believe that we as humans have the ability to continue to be cynical about all this. I guess we fear what we do not know or understand for the most part. Is it just our mind showing us what we want to hear or see? Or, is it something more than madness? What is madness? Could the ability or gift to sense, see, or hear life beyond our definition be madness in its purest form . . . or a single moment of intense clarity? I don't know for sure at this time, but I know what I experience with the dying in their final moments has certainly prompted me to search my heart and mind and become open to all possibilities.

Profound Peace

"Music expresses that which cannot be said and on which it is impossible to be silent."

Victor Hugo

As I came towards Gene's room, she lit up and called out, "Oh, look! It's the harp lady, come in, come in!" I walked into the room and greeted both Gene and her sister sitting in the chair beside her.

"Would you like some harp music today, ladies?" I said with a cheeky grin, knowing they were literally hanging out for some.

"Yes, please! We would love it, wouldn't we?" Gene said with a huge smile on her face that was covered by the tubes that ran from her nose towards an oxygen machine on her left. Gene was a young woman of around forty-five, and she had trouble breathing. I was not sure of her illness, and it did not matter, but she vaguely indicated lung cancer a couple of times.

Gene's sister ran over to the other side of the room to get a chair for me. She placed in at the foot of the bed, nice and close to them both.

"Bring it closer!" Gene said, waving her arms and motioning me forward. I slid the chair forward, and we all sat down in what ended up being a small circle between the three of us.

"What more could we want, ladies? Good company, music, and a lovely view from your window!" I commented.

"Indeed," Gene concurred.

"Now, ladies, I am very happy for you to continue chatting, as I do not want to interrupt your visit. I would not be offended in any way; in fact, it would be a privilege to play for you both."

"No, no, we are here to listen and relax." She glanced sideways at her sister with one eye open saying, "Don't say a word, okay?" She laid down the law as her sister smiled and proceeded to place one hand above her eye as if saluting her captain. It seemed amusing, to say the least.

I played for some time and found myself being able to connect well and move into the flow with much more ease than usual. I looked up from the harp strings to find Gene moving her arms around in the air, as if dancing in her seat or conducting an orchestra before her. It was as if she was touching clouds of light that I could not see, and all the while, her face was beaming with a smile from ear to ear. Her sister caught my eye, and she smiled, knowing how much Gene was enjoying this moment.

"Oh, I really am in heaven right now. This must be what heaven is like surely!" she said, and in one smooth movement, she removed the tubes coming from her nose. She waved, danced, and moved around in her chair as if a bird in flight, gracefully expressing the sounds of the harp and bringing the melodies to life.

As I began to complete the session and slowed the music, Gene moved her hands in front of her chest, placed them together as if in prayer, and then slid them slowly upward as if doing yoga. Her hands climbed upwards until they reached the pinnacle above her head, and there they stayed for the longest time as she sat in silence breathing normally and deeply. She then opened them out above her like a funnel.

If I closed my eyes, I am sure I could see bright white light beaming down in a stream through her hands into her entire body. The silence in the room was deafening, and the peace was indeed intense. Gene brought her hands back together, down the line of her body, and rested them on her heart. She remained for a moment and then took a long, deep breath. She opened her eyes and gazed towards me.

"Did you feel the profound peace fall upon us moment ago?" Gene said.

"Yes, I did, Gene, and it was beautiful," I said, finding it difficult to express myself in this perfect moment of peace.

"You know what? I had been in my pain all day," she said, "and for the first time in a long time, I feel deep peace within me, and also energy! I have not had energy for the longest time; I think I might even go for a walk!" she exclaimed and pushed aside the oxygen machine she relied on intently when I first walked into the room. The transformation was astounding, and I sat in awe at the amazing effect the music had on Gene. No longer was she gasping for every breath, she was filled with light that filled the room.

"Thank you, Angela, all of this is because of you. I am so grateful!"

I do not know how much of it is me or simply giving the gift of providing the environment for healing, but either way, it is such a privilege to be able to journey with these special people.

Debrief

> "A teacher affects eternity, he can never tell where his influence stops."
>
> **Henry Adams**

I feel that this chapter is in many ways the most important of all the work in this book. For without the skills outlined within, all the good work we do can often be negated by experiences that challenge us.

Cheryl Richardson says in her book, *The Unmistakable Touch of Grace*, that once in a while a spiritual change agent arrives in our lives. Some people have one, and others, like me, have many, depending on the context I am in. These people come into our lives to mark some kind of transition or significant change, helping us to let go of the old and birth the new. He or she is like a midwife, and the job at hand is to help us develop and express the talents we are meant to share, to assist us in transitioning through new phases of our lives, or to encourage us to awaken to the signs and gifts of grace.

My many midwives helped me give birth to my career as a healing musician. With their constant support, wise guidance, and unwavering encouragement, I have been able to fully step into this role with confidence and find a safe place to fall when I need it. And, as you have seen in some of the stories within this book, there are times when I genuinely needed it.

As much as this work is a privilege, profound, and life

changing, there are days, and patients, that test my resilience on every level. Like the layers of an onion, I feel as if many of my experiences I have with people on the wards are peeling back the layers of my soul and exposing the bare flesh for all to see. There are times when this is a painful process, yet it is a process that indeed must be experienced to be complete. I am now learning it does not have to be painful, just a gentle allowing of life to happen around me without the usual resistance. The resistance to what is happening is what causes the pain. So, it is simple. Just let it be and flow with the energy of life trusting that it will indeed take me exactly where I need to go.

I have had days when I have overheard people saying: "There goes that harp woman again, she drives me mad!" or "Does she have to come in here and play for us? It is jarring!" or even better, "You are torturing me!" And with every experience I am finding I am spending less time in turmoil and more time in acceptance and understanding, finding my center once again.

There are days when it feels as if going back onto the wards with my harp would be the last thing I would ever want to do, all the result of a single bad experience. Then I would be graced with a person who has told me that my playing has changed his life, made her day, or brought him to a place of such peace that he forgot he was in hospital. It is a tension of opposites, and understanding this tension is my goal in every moment.

I now understand that it is not about me, also that each person I interact with is coming from his place of perception, learning, and understanding of what is good, relaxing, and peaceful. And sometimes they are resisting everything that just might remind them of something they need to address, let go of, or accept, if they let their guard down for one moment, I might just get in. And sometimes I do. In all of the hundreds of bedside sessions I have given, there have only been a handful of what one could say negative experiences, which is pretty good odds. The problem is that one never knows when someone is going to react to the harp, the music, or me, for whatever reason, their subconscious decides there is a conflict. Because I do not know, and I cannot control the actions of others, it is important for me to learn how to control my own actions, and reactions to others, and then deal with the residue of the suppressed feelings if there are any.

Suppressed feelings and emotions are, I believe, an important factor in total well-being and health. The more we suppress our feelings, the more our subconscious will try to alert us by creating physical symptoms. So the need for self-care and the opportunity to debrief your day with someone is a gift, and remember not to take it home with you, deal with it in the moment.

There have been days when I have had a stressful bedside and not knowing how to express what I had experienced I would be met by my supporters with clarity and wisdom, always finding a way to defuse the emotional pain and re-center.

The greatest gift any human being can give to others is to help them find their way back to the love that resides inside them.

A typical debriefing session would proceed as follows:

Outline the experience; explain the circumstance or situation to a supporter. It is good to have this person prearranged and ready to help when you need a sounding board. This is a person who will not feed your reaction, will remain objective, and help you find the greater truth in it all rather than just adding to what could be a destructive mental story about it. (Typically, our story is much worse than the reality.)

Speak about how you felt about it and what you are feeling in the moment, fully accepting it, and embracing it as best you can.

A supporter could then acknowledge your pain, especially if the pain was the result of someone else's thoughtless actions. This is important as even though we do eventually come to the place where we own what is ours, and ask ourselves why we have had such a reaction to this person; it is always appropriate to acknowledge someone's pain so they can experience it and move to the next level.

A supporter may then ask the difficult questions like: What subconscious belief is this uncovering for you? What is this patient mirroring back to you? Sometimes it might be the belief that everyone has to like me, or everyone rejects me, or the big one, I am not good enough, etc. Usually once I have moved through my own emotional battlefield, on the other side of it all I find clarity of what it is truly about for me. Any reaction I have to someone or something is always an issue that is living within me that has been triggered. For if it were not there, I would not have reacted in the first place.

I also use techniques I have learned from reading Byron Katie's book, *Loving What Is*. If you have not read this book, I wholeheartedly recommend you do. It has been a powerful tool and helps to shine a light on the story the mind tells us about something or a situation and stops it in its tracks.

The basic questions I ask myself in any stressful situation are:

Is it true? Can I absolutely know that it is true? (Believe me, nine times out of ten, the story we have been telling ourselves about someone or something isn't actually true when we get down to it.) How do you react when you believe the thought? How do you treat the person involved when you attach to that belief? How do you treat yourself? Who or what would you be without the thought? Now, turn your statement around. (Can you find three genuine examples of how the turnaround is as true or even truer in your life?)

If you only ever use the question "Is it true?" as a tool for empowerment in your life, your life will transform before your eyes as you step fully into reality and truth. The fact is that we cannot fight reality; it is when we do that we suffer.

Another technique learned from Byron Katie I use in many situations in my life and work as a healing musician is to remember the following. There are three types of business in the world. There is my business, your business, and God's business only to consider.

My business is what I choose to do, and that is my business and mine alone. Then there is your business, which is what you choose to do, react to and experience. I have no business being in yours and vice versa. Then there is God's business. This is the stuff we just cannot control, the weather, traffic, etc.

I cannot tell you in words how powerful this simple information is, and has been, for me. The moment you find yourself in someone else's business, get out of it! While you are busy dabbling in their lives, who is in yours? Not you, that is for sure. Stay in your own business! It is as simple as that, and life will become so effortless, so easy and blissful you will be astounded.

Another important piece of information I will share with you that has helped me on my journey as a healing musician and in general life is this. How do I know something or anything in life for that matter was meant to happen? Because it is! It happened! How can we question what is? You cannot fight reality. When we do, we suffer. This realization literally transformed my life and brought peace beyond my imagination in so many areas of my existence. I dare you to give it a try.

I also study Eckhart Tolle's teachings on present moment awareness. This is extremely powerful in this line of work for more reasons than one.

Once you have found the bliss and relief in each of these tools, there is then the profound work of Dr. Ihaleakala Hew Len and his powerful practice called Ho'oponopono.

Simply put, Ho'oponopono means "to make right." It is an ancient Hawaiian method of clearing ourselves and thoughts that have been tainted by painful memories from the past. It offers a simple way to release the energy or errors that cause imbalance and disease.

This process, of all the self development work I have ever done in my life, has been the most immediate, powerful, and peace giving, requiring the full responsibility of everything in our lives. A concept that may first feel difficult quickly becomes effortless and a wonderful journey of revealing the true you and your most wondrous life as you continually release, polishing the mirror of your soul to reveal a luminous being.

In this we are reminded that what you see in another is also in you, so all healing is essentially self healing. In the end, no one else has to do these processes but you, the entire world then being in your hands.

Whenever you find yourself in a position where something is happening that you know you like, upsets you, or triggers an emotional response, Dr. Hew Len teaches us to first say "I am sorry, please forgive me" to acknowledge that something has gotten into our subconscious system, you may not even know how. You don't need to know why, but by saying "I'm sorry," you are telling the divine that you seek forgiveness within you. It is good to remember we are not asking the divine for forgiveness, we are asking the divine to help forgive ourselves.

From there you would then say "Thank you" and "I love you." When you say "thank you," you are expressing gratitude and showing faith that the issue will be resolved for the highest good of all concerned. The "I love you" transmutes the energy from stuck to flowing, and as such, it reconnects you to the divine.

Just a few hints….. Good luck, and if all else fails, remember to BREATHE.

The Final
Graceful Passage

"For a moment they hover like bejeweled clouds, and
dance above the crystal streams,
Then, as they sail away on the laughing waters, they
seem to say:
Farewell, O spring we are on to eternity."

Okakura Kakuzo

To complete this book I would like to share my experience with a brave young woman dying of cancer. I spent countless hours with this woman who seemed so accepting of her situation. I would play harp for her, and for what seemed like hours, we would talk. Talk about everything. She was so open, so vital, and so accepting of her situation, even though at times she was puzzled as to why. Ironically enough though, she was happy not to know, her way reminds me of a story someone shared with me recently about his experience of meeting the Dali Lama. During question time, someone asked, "Why do bad things happen to good people?" The Dali Lama answered with a short: "God knows! Next question"

The most important thing I have learned over the past two years of doing this work is that the music is just the key. A key to allowing the patient to relax, release, pass on, express themselves, or just talk. It is a key, or a tool, like any other art that aids the unfolding of the soul. The last time I saw her I told her about the fact I would like to share her story someday in a book. The intention of this book is to honor her and others through the art of storytelling in the hope it might just make a difference to someone else facing the same situation. I nervously asked her if there was one thing she could tell people about life and death, one thing she could say about her experience of living and dying, one piece of advice she could give, what would it be.

As she was now extremely weak and finding it difficult to find the energy to communicate, she closed her eyes and began to speak as if searching for an answer from some deep well of wisdom she had access to.

"Tell them to live their life, enjoy it, love it, and most importantly, be grateful. I spent most of my life unhappy about things, depressed, feeling sorry for myself about not having enough money, support, love, or whatever, and now look at me. Now, I have something to be sad about. Now, I am truly running out of time. Time to breathe, time to laugh, time to see sunsets, and time to be with those I love. All of the so-called things that were so very important to me now are like dust on the breeze, leaving only what truly matters, existence. I am leaving my two daughters; this is a tragedy. To think I believed that a tragedy was not paying my bills or not having lots of money. What a waste.

"Perception is everything. Do you know that each day of my life I walked along the beach in the afternoon? I would walk and then sit on the sand for hours feeling sorry for myself. Why? In that moment, I had it all. I just could not see it. Believe me, dying focused the lens of my reality more than any other experience I have ever had, and I see now what my life truly was. I had health, I had the love of my children, I had food in my belly, I had a lovely home and a job, and more than this, I had the beauty of nature all around me. What I would give right now to go outside and take one last breath of fresh air, it would be like being in paradise. When we are rushing around in our lives, we forget to breathe, we forget to be grateful for the little things in life, and we forget to enjoy the sweet taste of fresh, clean air.

"The gift of every single breath we take. I have been in this room for months now, the air is stale, and I would give anything to sit in the sun and breathe, but now the light is too much for me, and I need to be here in the darkened room. In my past, breathing was something I just did without even considering its immense power, but now I count each precious one like a grain of golden sand passing through the hourglass of my life. I suggest you do the same as you never know when the portal of life and death will open for you, my friend.

"It is difficult to explain what this situation is like; I would not like you to understand as for you to understand you would need to follow my footsteps. This situation is hard. The pain is so intense that I want to scream and scream, but there is no energy to even whisper.

"Why is the suffering in this world so great and why are people so ungrateful for all they have when they have it? It is like we are all blind, sleepwalking through life. Trust me when I say I am wide awake these days. Please tell them to wake up and be grateful and enjoy every second. Look at me, only a few months ago I was just like you, worried, rushing around, living my life, and now I struggle because my family wants me to fight to live, but the time for acceptance has come. If only I found this acceptance in life, I may not be here accepting my death just yet, but I am. To be honest, I would love to have a needle that would help me to disappear and escape this agonizing, unimaginable pain, but it would upset my family, and so I hang on for them until the end. But for all the pain it would bring my family, I would gladly die today, because the pain is so great," she said with tears rolling down her face.

"Tell them not to be afraid to die. There is nothing to fear, it is just another dimension we are all going to, that is all. It's very natural, like birth, and yet why are we all so afraid to do it?" She turned to me with eyes filled with tears and said, "I am so sorry I cannot hear the music today, as even to communicate is difficult, and even the sound of my own voice is irritating. Sound is irritating for me. Everything is being stripped from me. Everything I think I am until I am nothing, or am I becoming everything? Everything that this world is not, the great I AM all. I know not."

I asked her one more question, knowing she was growing weary and realizing our time together that day was almost up. "I find it hard to know what I can do to help you, what to say, how can others help people like you?" She smiled and said, "I have been hoping you would ask. Look in my drawer and take out the sheet that is there. Someone gave it to me and it is the closest expression of how I feel and how I think you can help. All I ask is that you remember that your presence alone is enough and that even until the final moment and beyond we are living."

We said what would be our final goodbyes, and I found the letter. I folded it up, put it in my pocket, and left her to again rest. This was the last time I would see this special lady, though her words are living within me, and now within you. The letter read:

Dear Friend,
This is how you can help me. Don't tell me that you understand, don't tell me that you know, and don't tell me that I will survive how I will surely grow. Don't tell me this is just a test, that I am truly blessed, that I am chosen for this task, apart from all the rest. Don't come at me with answers that can come from only me, don't tell me how my grief will pass, that I will soon be free. Don't stand in pious judgment, of the bonds I must un-tie, don't tell me how to suffer, don't tell me how to cry. My life is filled with selfishness; my pain is all I see. But I need you; I need your love unconditionally. Accept me in my ups and downs, I need someone to share. Just hold my hand and let me cry, and say, "my friend, I'm here."

Full Circle

aving you read these words, hear these stories, and flip these pages has been a dream of mine for many years. After countless additions, deletions, and reworks, this book has finally come full circle and has been joyfully birthed into this world.

For most of my life I have been bestowed with the so-called gift of blind faith, a dreamer's heart, and a restless mind that is regularly told to "grow up" and get a real job. I clarify this by saying I have never been told this by anyone but myself. How could I ever become an author? I could see no way how, but the way was made.

Over the years things happen, hearts are broken, and dreams seem lost. I am sure you can relate to the moment when one decides that dreams do not come true, and magic doesn't really happen. Well, at least it doesn't happen to people like me.

I will never forget the day the final mile of the journey of birthing this book began. I was invited to attend a meditation with some of my nearest and dearest friends in the Blue Mountains, not unlike many other meditation days that we have embarked on in our long friendship.

It was a beautiful day. Good friends, good food, and powerful moments of peace were experienced while we relaxed to a mediation named "Transformation" (Maureen Moss). I must take this moment to thank Amanda for finding these meditations and sharing them with us, and Rosemary, for providing a beautiful space for us all to enjoy each other's company and grow.

This meditation, not unlike others I have listened to in the past, focused us on allowing life to happen effortlessly and in a transformative way. Rather than wasting our time and energy on worry, stress, and the act of striving for something, we are encouraged to embrace that which life offers to us, and in that there lies the key. When we totally and lovingly embrace that which is in our life, all that we are meant to be, do, and have will come to us naturally and with joy and ease. The words that rang in my ears as Joanne, my dear friend, and I left the meditation was "it will be handed to you."

Joanne had invited me to attend a doTERRA Essential Oil event on the central coast as a supporter, both of us being independent product consultants for this conscious company that sells and promotes healthy living through the use of essential oils. I had no idea what I was meant to do at this event apart from possibly sitting at a table and chat with passersby about doTERRA's special Certified Pure Therapeutic Grade essential oils. I thought to myself that regardless of the long drive, and lack of energy, I would enjoy the trip with Joanne and another friend, Deb.

To be honest, after my last attempt at editing the book I had not thought about it for quite some time, and it was certainly not on my mind the day I was led to the publisher that would eventually see something in the string of words I had put together on these pages.

I had sent my book out to many publishers and received similar responses from each, that it was not really their "thing," and therefore not to be picked up for publishing. I came to a point in my journey with the book that it felt so finished that I didn't really feel the need to ever even read it again. By the time the day came that made it clear there might just be a chance it could be published, I had completely let go of the dream and was ready to put it in my file marked "complete."

Joanne, Deb, and I arrived at our venue on the central coast, unloaded the car, and began to set up our beautiful oil display for the attendees to view. It just so happened that Joanne decided to sit me right next to a lady named Melissa. Melissa would prove to be the key to it all. I sat behind my table for a few moments relaxing, and eventually I decided it would be a nice idea to introduce Melissa at the table beside me to the oils. We chatted for a while, and I eventually purchased a silver ring from Melissa's table that Joanne could not keep her eyes off all night. It was quite funny actually to see the delight in Joanne's eyes when she saw this ring with the inscription "Be the change you wish to see in the world." Back and forward she would come, looking at the ring, and then putting it down with a sigh.

I turned to Melissa and said, "May I please buy that silver ring there, but do me a favor and don't tell Joanne, as I would like to surprise her." Melissa agreed, so I put the ring in my pocket to present to Joanne later that night. I decided we could kill two birds with one stone. I could be the change I wished to see in the world, and Joanne could then be inspired to do the same. The meaning and love layered onto this gift mounted high.

Moments later, Joanne came back to again covert the ring that had now disappeared, both Melissa and I holding back giggles as Joanne noticed it was gone and asked Melissa if she could order it. Of course Melissa tried her best to encourage Joanne to email her later with her order. In that moment, I felt life was showing me a great lesson, that sometimes we already have what we desire, we just don't know it yet, and to just relax, be patient, and enjoy the moment of pure possibility. The other lesson was not to feel sad when we think we have missed out on something, as often, it is not the case and all we need is to trust that either we were spared something by not receiving it, or it is still on its way.

Once the fun had settled down, Melissa and I began a conversation about the book that lay on her table. We exchanged business cards, and it was then things became interesting. We chatted for the rest of the evening about her interest in having me play the harp for a new project she was working on that involved me playing intuitive music to accompany wording in her already written book. Melissa gifted me with a copy of her book and asked me to get a feel for it so that we may meet up at a later date to go over some ideas.

Curious, I asked Melissa about her journey to becoming a published author, and her answer left me gob smacked. "It was just handed to me," she said with tears in her eyes. She had written this beautiful work and then had a friend take a look at it. Her friend encouraged her to pitch it to some publishers, so she did. Melissa, like many other literary hopefuls, received the usual response "thanks, but no thanks" from all of the publishers except one. This publisher told her that it wasn't really their thing, but they encouraged her to try another publisher that may just like it.

Well, the rest is history, and six months later, Melissa had a beautifully published book on her doorstep. "It was all so easy and effortless," she explained, "I don't really know how it happened, to be honest."

Meanwhile, I sat with my jaw on the floor, as so much of what Melissa said to me was almost word for word what the meditation had encouraged us would happen if we could just relax and allow life to come to us. Just show up for your life, take the opportunities that come to you, and the rest will take care of itself.

I told Melissa I had a book of stories I would love to publish and she encouraged me to contact her publisher, the one that has published the very book you now hold in your hands. So I took her details, the details of the publisher, and I set out to meet life halfway and do as she suggested, even though everything in me still believed it was not possible someone would see in my work something worth publishing.

That night, Joanne, Deb, and I were abuzz with energy and excitement with just the synchronicity of that day and evening. "Imagine if I actually got a publishing deal," I mused. We all laughed and joked the whole way home, even though it was late at night, we were all tired and in need of sleep, we basked in the journey of the day and enjoyed the moment filled with possibility.

I guess considering you are now reading these words, you know what happened next. The publisher said yes, and the magic that is life reminded me that sometimes when we dream deeply, work diligently, apply ourselves and just turn up in our lives, anything can happen. Magic does happen, and I encourage you to take that to heart and enjoy your dreams, but remember to let them go so that they may go out into the world and come back to you. Sometimes we hold onto our dreams so hard that they cannot grow. Just relax and trust that in the most humble moment in life awaits the key you have been waiting for to the chest of treasure you have been seeking.

I complete this work by contemplating many questions around this day and its outcome. What if I decided not to go to the meditation that day? What if I decided I was too tired to go with Joanne to the central coast? What if Joanne did not even ask me to go? What if I sat somewhere else, and I did not meet Melissa? What if Melissa decided not to go that evening? The latter could have happened as Melissa was not feeling well at the time, but thankfully, a quick application of one of doTERRA's fast acting oils, and she was feeling much better.

There are so many what-ifs in life in general, and if this story teaches me anything it is that no matter what, if something is meant to be, the way will be made. Maybe not in our time, but it will come eventually in the still, small, insignificant moments when we least expect it.

And so it is in the still, small, significant moment that is now. A lazy day in spring that I trust I am right where I am meant to be, and so are you.

Thank you.

Thank you

Deep thanks to all those seen and unseen who lovingly played a part in the manifestation of this book. Those past, present, and future, to each and every one of you who I have sat with at the bedside I honor you. This book is for you.

Thank you to my family and friends who lovingly supported me always and never lost faith in who I am and what I do.

Thank you to the publisher, editors, and designers. Thank you for seeing something in my work worth sharing with the world. Thank you Renee for helping to make the text sparkle with your new found love of editing. I am so grateful for your assistance.

To my beloved husband, Steve. Without your love and support, I would not have been freed to do all that I do, so thank you so much.

After years of writing, putting it away, and being gently reminded over and over again that it was waiting to be birthed into this world—it is finished—or has it just begun?

Bibliography

M. Stillwater, Remal Malkin, *Graceful Passages. A Companion for Living and Dying.* (Companion Arts Music, 2003)

Benson, Stella (CMP). *The Healing Musician: A Guide to Playing Healing Music at the Bedside.* (New Grail Publishing, 1999)

Richardson, Cheryl. *The Unmistakeable Touch of Grace: How to Recognize and Respond the Spiritual Signposts in your Life.* (Free Press, New York, 2005)

Briggs, Tami. *Reflections on the Harp and Healing.* (Musical Reflections Press, 2002)

Barbato, Michael. *Caring for the Dying.* (McGraw-Hill Medical, 2002)

Albom, Mitch. *Tuesdays with Morrie: An Old Man, a Young Man, and Life's Greatest Lessons.* (Hodder, Australia, 1998)